110 MILES WITH JESUS

A Prayer Journey and Journal

Marlo Coker

ISBN 979-8-89428-597-9 (paperback)
ISBN 979-8-89428-598-6 (digital)

Copyright © 2024 by Marlo Coker

All rights reserved. No part of this publication may be reproduced, distributed, or transmitted in any form or by any means, including photocopying, recording, or other electronic or mechanical methods without the prior written permission of the publisher. For permission requests, solicit the publisher via the address below.

Christian Faith Publishing
832 Park Avenue
Meadville, PA 16335
www.christianfaithpublishing.com

Printed in the United States of America

I have some amazing, awesome, stupendous people in my life! It would be hard to name them ALL. Here are the ones that have helped this work of art (the book and me) come to life.

I have had the privilege to serve under three Pastors in the twenty-four years I've known Christ:

Bishop James E Varnum and his son Pastor Jason Varnum of Souls Harbor First Pentecostal Church, Belleview, Florida, both taught me the importance of salvation, how to truly get ahold of God, and stay when you're supposed to stay, move when you're supposed to move.

Pastor Barry Dotson of the Rock Church, Blairsville, Georgia, taught me how to be okay with being isolated, how to seek the Lord on my own without relying on accompaniment and how to go deeper in the word and to linger in His presence.

Pastor Joe Guinta of Detroit Hope Center, Detroit, Michigan, has been my pastor for just a short time but he and his wife have been a friend, a leader, and an example of how to truly love people for almost the same amount of time as I've been saved. His family has demonstrated how to persevere and how to rise up.

Family and Friends are a precious and wonderful gift that should not be taken for granted.

To my husband, Kevin Coker, who has loved and supported every crazy journey and has had a few of his own. Has held the steering wheel as I wrote notes for this book and drove (because it was my turn) in order to keep a thought. Who has been my life partner and prayer partner and helps keep me on my knees while I help keep him on his toes!

To my boys, who most likely wish to remain anonymous, even though they probably won't read this, I appreciate their tolerance of me writing about intimate situations of our family and my thoughts about those situations.

To all my friends, who have taken a call as I was driving so I could vent, gain wisdom, and spit ideas and dreams at:

Teresa Billingsley
Stacy Fager
Laura Amundson
Abigail Earnheart
Gina Lamarre
Melissa Lesage

Contents

Lilies of the Field 1
Clinical Questions in Spiritual Form 3
In the Beginning 7
Put a Pin in It..9
Open Up the Floodgates 11
Are You Not Entertained?!....................................13
Sssshhhhh 15
Lessons from the Car Wash 17
Armor of God 19
The Gates of Hell..21
Sour Grapes..23
Hide-and-Seek 25
Ewwww!..27
Time For a Test 29
It Is Finished? 31
Fruits of the Spirit..33
Love 37
Joy..41
Peace 43
Gentleness and Meekness 47
Long-suffering..49
Why Am I Like This? 53
Goodness 55
Church Hurt..57
Pay Attention 59
I'm So Mad Today, God! 61
Sinews..65
Which Way?..67
Faith..69
Temperance..71
Rejoice with Me! 73
Graduation-Gradually Gravitating Upward 75
Judges..77

Porters...81
You've Been Subitized...83
I Am for You, Not against You..............................85
Lazarus, Come Forth!..87
Down to Your Level 89
Hyperboles..91
Shibboleth...93
The Gospel Series..95
Four Words 99
This Is How We Drive 103
What's the Difference?...105
Onomatopoeia 107
Praying Through the Temple 109
Fasting While Praying Through the Temple.........113
Absence Makes the What Do What? 115
Get Your House Ready 117
How Much Longer? 119
Time to Get Uncomfortable................................121
Look at Me!...123
God Is on the Move 127
Withhold Nothing 129
God Roar 131
Entertaining Angels Unaware 133
Don't Be Afraid of Their Faces............................135
Thy Will 137

Lilies of the Field

Consider the lilies how they grow: they toil not, they spin not; and yet I say unto you, that Solomon in all his glory was not arrayed like one of these. If then God so clothe the grass, which is to day in the field, and to morrow is cast into the oven; how much more will he clothe you, O ye of little faith?

—Luke 12:27–28

A Word from the author, GOD

This book was written for YOU. Every topic was designed to help YOU and YOUR situation. I have used a vessel to speak to You. I give YOU and others valleys and mountains to walk through so that YOU can be a light to those who need it. YOU WILL come out of your valley. YOU WILL climb mountains.

YOU WILL be able to show others how to keep their head up as they walk the same path you just traveled. Do not discount MY word, MY promises to YOU.

Do not question the delivery of MY word.
I have used
 A rock
  A donkey
   A mud ball (several)
    Water (several ways)
     I WILL use you.
You are my resource. Let me extract the good parts of you.
You are my light. Shine in this dark world so that they see me.
You are the salt of the Earth. Go flavor those that are bland.

A word from the vessel, Me

I now know how the authors of the Bible felt. I'm not being haughty. In fact, it's quite humbling and scary to say that God gave me all these words for the purpose of helping others. To have the responsibility that it's to His satisfaction is scary and beautiful. Every word in this devotional has come through either a Bible study that has been taught or a lesson God showed me during times in my "isolation" (a.k.a. my car).

He has given me each one of these topics to write about for the purpose of helping someone or a group of someone.

Topics started on a blank page with the Lord using my fingers as his own utensil. As I was driving on a long drive, he said, "Write about this" and "Write about that," as I was trying to keep track of all the topics in a note on my phone so I could write about them later has turned into beautiful, poetic, anecdotal, funny, and even heart-wrenching (as I've had to relive some hurtful moments) devotional pages for you to read, learn, study and grow.

I have truly prayed over each page. Praying that it helps someone who is feeling exactly how I have felt. If nothing else, I pray that it has encouraged you to journal your own thoughts and experiences with Jesus.

Sincerely,
Marlo Coker

Clinical Questions in Spiritual Form

As a new clinician, if I have learned anything from my studies in this field, I have learned to ask what, how, and why. If we are to ask those questions in science and in specific professions, it's only fair to ask God and ourselves those same questions when it comes to our relationship with him.

Everything in heaven and earth has been made by him. He has all the answers we need, so why not ask him?

What?

What is this book about? It's about making you realize that it's okay to question God if it's in the right spirit. It's about being real with God because he's real with us. He directs our pastors and leaders to be real with us in every service, through every sermon. It's all done out of love, but it's real, and it's for the purpose of creating a relationship with God. He is real with us in the written word. He's real with us in his audible/internal voice that he whispers or screams to get our attention. This book is about going deeper into the word, deeper into your thoughts, and deeper into real-life situations and the reality of your feelings about those real-life situations.

Most importantly, creating a deeper relationship with HIM!

WHY?

I have learned to LOVE the word of God—the Holy Bible, the RoadMap to Life, the Source of Life. I haven't always loved it. I found it hard to read and understand, especially in the KJV. I found it hard to hear certain characteristics of God: his anger, his rage. However, as I have delved deeper into HIS word over the last few years, I have found an absolute, insatiable love for the living, fluid word of God. I found a love that God has for his people. The anger and the rage come out of frustration of constantly seeing his people turn their backs on him.

Yes, he still loves us. I see his love in humanity and his love through the word in everyday life. I hear it in random conversations. Just as a musician and songwriter hears notes, tones, and lyrics in everyday occurrences, I hear and see THE WORD in everything. The word has been how I understand God in my personal walk with him.

This is why this book was created.

I want you to journey with me and God.

I want you to be a part of walking in the cool of the garden.

I want you to walk or drive with him on your own!

How do you dissect your Bible? What do you do to bring yourself closer to his word?

How?

How do you use this book?
However, you want.
Read it through once and then put it down.
Pick it back up at a later time.
See progress in yourself and your relationship each time.
Like the Bible, it is meant to be used over and over.
It is meant to be written in highlighted.
Used as lesson plans and life applications. Cry in it. Pray in it.
> Read it in the morning.
> Read it in the evening.
> Read it on road trips.
> Read it back to front,
> Front to back,
> From middle to front,
> End to middle,
> Middle to End
> Give it away if you see fit.

The content on the pages was not created in the same time period.
Each section was not created for the same purpose as the next.
Each page has a different purpose.
There is no rhyme or reason to the order of these pages.
You're a smart cookie, you get it.
There are no rules to how you use it.
> Use it as your journal.
> Use it as a daily/weekly devotional.
> Use it for inspiration.
> Use it to write your own story.
> Use it to find hope.
> Use it to write your own testimonies.

There are journaling lines after each topic, but don't limit yourself to those lines. There are also intentional blank pages for your notes and your thoughts and for you to write scriptures that are inspiring and relatable to you and your story.

In the Beginning

I love to travel. Staying in one place is difficult at times. My upbringing created that in me. I believe this is why I tend to hear God's voice more while driving than at other times. I am no stranger to car rides with Jesus. Before I knew Christ (really knew him), I knew the form of him but not WHO he was. I was trying to decide if I was going to stay in a dysfunctional marriage with two small boys, trying to decide if we were going to buy a house in California and work it out or buy a house in Florida and work it out—or not. Maybe I would leave for Florida without him. I'm so thankful Jesus showed up "before I was (re)born" because he knew me. He knew my husband before we were reborn. He knew who we would be together.

He showed up…

> …in my car, right there in the passenger seat. His form was there, his voice was there.

He was there.

Every time I tell this story, I think back and realize that, surprisingly, I wasn't even startled by his very real presence. Kind of like when the angels appeared out of nowhere in the Bible and said, **"Be not afraid."**

Somehow, I had already recognized his form and his presence as if he had been a passenger in my car the whole time.

Anyway, there I was, lost in thought, and there he was.

Me: What am I going to do? I have to make a decision…something needs to change.

God: Go to Florida with your husband. I will lead your path. I will be with you. I will not leave you.

It took a while to find him in Florida, but we did. His promise was true. He was there, guiding our feet. He still is.

"Thy word is a lamp unto my feet, and a light unto my path" (Psalm 119:105).

110 MILES WITH JESUS

Where do you find God in unexpected places?

Shameless plug, find the rest of that story in *Jesus Stole My Weed!: A Testimony of Substance Abuse Freedom (and Other Life-Altering Stories)* by Kevin and Marlo Coker!

Put a Pin in It

I see you, Lord. I see where you have been in my life. Sometimes just here and there and sometimes long stretches of time. **I see you!**

"I see you too. I see you before you were formed in your mother's womb. I see you now. I see you as you take your last breath while I rock you and then welcome you into the kingdom. The true kingdom that I have already prepared for you. I see you. Then, Now, Later."

I imagine God showing up in my life as one can look at a national or world map with pins in it. I can look back on my life and see exactly where he has had his hand on my life, even when I didn't know who he was. I wouldn't have even been able to tell you that God existed in some of those moments, in the moment. But I look back now, and I can tell you THE EXACT MOMENT when God showed up. I can tell you one of the multiple times of depression and attempted suicide when a priest walked right up to me when NOBODY else was around as I was contemplating another method for death.

He simply asked if I was okay, and with little response from me, he simply said, "God will take care of you," and walked away. It interrupted my thoughts and my actions at that moment.

There were other times when I could pinpoint his presence without my knowledge. I have always felt I was being "watched" as a little girl, and there were times that it scared me. Knowing better now, I wish I would have embraced it more. No matter, he was there. That is the important part. He was a pin in so many times of my life. If I had a map of my time line, it would be completely covered in pins. How I love the fact that he cared for me that much! Just think about the vast number of people in the world and that he does the same thing for each of us. He's with YOU now! He's in this room and in your room. He is OMNIPRESENT.

110 MILES WITH JESUS

Where do you KNOW God has shown up in your life?

Open Up the Floodgates

I don't have a writer's block problem. I have a floodgate problem. I feel like I am constantly creating a narrative in my mind. Or God is doing the narrating and I'm doing the listening.

Although, I don't feel like I'm a typical writer. I don't write down or jot all my thoughts onto paper. I use my Bible as my journal. I carry note cards and my Bible everywhere with me, and when I feel like something is parallel to scripture, which everything is parallel to scripture, I find that place and write a note or highlight that verse in my Bible. If the word is deeper or more expandable into other scriptures, I use my note cards to help the main ideas come into place. My Bible is messy. It has notes on almost every page, and it has note cards in most books. Water has spilled onto it (ashamedly, SEVERAL times). Sacrileges, right? Writing, spilling, and ruining THE HOLY WORD.

Wait, isn't that what it's for? The scripture says to study to show thyself approved. When you study something, don't you highlight, make notes, or chop up the information until it makes sense? Late-night study sessions to divulge the word (and snacks)—cram sessions—sometimes get messy!

My Bible was made for all of that and more. It does not mean that I dishonor his Word. In fact, quite the opposite, I adore it so much, I want it involved in everything I do, including munching and sipping—ooops.

When I listen to songs, it's with me.

I write notes in my Bible that correlate with song lyrics.

When I listen to preaching and the speaker says turn with me to, I immediately think of ten other scriptures that correlate to the opening lines or a situation that previously brought me to that specific passage.

I am not being disrespectful when my pages flip like crazy as I search for meaningful context of what a speaker is preaching. I'm finding inspiration and respecting the message that God gave them and applying a currently spoken word and previously spoken word with the written word.

My mind is always pointing to the practical application of the word.

"But be ye doers of the word, and not hearers only."

How do you use your Bible? How do you feel inspired to go deeper in the word?

_____
_____
_____
_____
_____
_____
_____
_____
_____
_____
_____
_____
_____

Are You Not Entertained?!

This is a line from the movie *Gladiator*. I have never seen the movie but I've heard the quote several times in my life. This is what God spoke to me one early morning on my drive to work. At the time, I was driving sixty miles one way. That's a 110-mile round trip each day, not including other duties throughout the day, but you get the point—it was a lot of time in my car. I had done this for several months and would spend about ten minutes of prayer as I first drove off into darkness. Then I would spend another fifteen minutes listening to the Bible chapters. I checked the boxes of my Christian duty, and then I would turn on the radio to bebop my way to work the rest of the time, listening to Godly, holy, sanctified Christian music.

There and back, there and back, there and back. Day in, day out, day in, day out, nothing is flooding my ears with garbage. All is right here, Lord.

GOD: Are you worshipping me or just being entertained?

ME. What? It's CHRISTIAN MUSIC. You put it into the writers and the musicians. I'm worshipping YOU!

GOD: Are you worshipping me or just being entertained? (He usually has to ask me the same question twice to get me to admit the answer that he already knows.)

ME: I'm being entertained WHILE worshipping you (question mark)? (He'll be satisfied with that answer! I'm sure of it)

GOD: Turn it off. (Period)

ME: Ooohhhkaayyyy (insert proverbial eye roll)!

GOD: Now you will hear me and worship me properly.

From that day on, my radio stays off as I'm driving (for the most part). When I feel like singing, he puts a song in my heart to sing to him. Sometimes, he will let me use YouTube if I only know the title or chorus but not the lyrics. If you've ever heard my singing voice, you'll understand that God is relieved that I use YouTube.

110 MILES WITH JESUS

If I am allowed to listen to Christian radio on a long drive, such as XM The Message, it's only for a short period, and I thank him for the allotment.

Most days were not filled with song though. Most days were filled with his word, spoken and written. Visions and direction are given during those times. Bible studies are birthed.

Prayers for my friends and family are birthed. Tears are shed. This book's concept was created because of those times.

Where can you go to hear his voice?

_____

_____

_____

_____

_____

_____

_____

How much time each day can you devote to him?

_____

_____

_____

_____

_____

_____

Sometimes, it's just sitting silent with him, and other times, you may want to pour out your whole heart. Where can you find five minutes, one hour, three hours each day to be with him?

_____

_____

_____

_____

_____

Sssshhhhh

Do you hear it?
Silence.
Is it deafening?
Or is it refreshing?
When we block all of the environmental noises
We can hear his voice.
So loud and clear.
In those moments,
he gives us direction,
comforts us, appeals to us.
Stop and listen
to the still
small voice
of our SAVIOR
HIGHER
UP
CALLING YOU to come

LISTEN…what do you hear him saying to you?

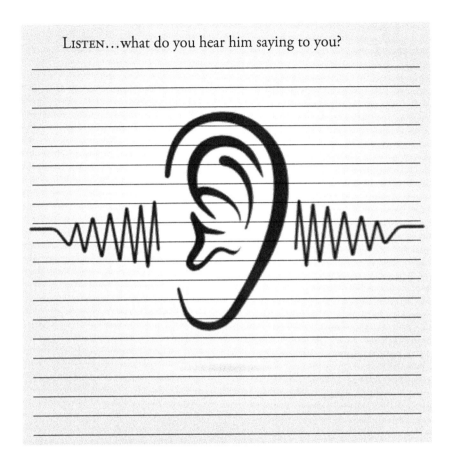

Lessons from the Car Wash

- The vacuums are more powerful than they seem (sucked my skirt up while male employees watched and laughed).
- You don't realize how dirty your vehicle is until you start cleaning it.
- Once it's clean, you start seeing specks of dirt everywhere. Even days after, you make grave attempts to keep it clean, at least for a little while.
- The idea of trusting and getting into the automated track is scary and creates unsurety of letting go of control.
- If you put your vehicle in reverse before putting it into neutral, as you move forward (no matter how slowly) on the automated track, you get to see all perspectives of the process with the backup camera.

Where do you see biblical principles and life applications in everyday occurrences?

Spiritual Perspectives from the car wash...

This world will suck you in faster than you expect it to. People will watch as you struggle, even laugh and mock you. Do not be discouraged; if they're going to watch you fail, make sure that they also watch you pick yourself back up and succeed!

Yes, you're dirty. So am I. When we get ourselves cleaned up, even if it's incomplete, we realize how dirty we actually were.

Then we want to stay clean. We start to recognize the slightest spot and wrinkle and want to perfect it.

You will never get so clean that it will be perfect. Jesus wants us to strive for perfection.

He wants our efforts. Our desires. Our improvements. That's what makes us perfect in his eyes.

Ah, trust. Trusting him that he is in control and our progress is at his speed. It's so hard to take your hands off the steering wheel and feet off the pedals, but the reward for doing so is SO SWEET! When we let go of control, we are blessed with miracles!

Look back, not to create a desire for something that was but...

...to see the process...

...to see the progress of your journey.

Look back and look to each side... See all the perspectives.

Armor of God

Ephesians 6:10–20 says that we are not fighting flesh and blood. We are fighting the spirits of this world. When someone says or does something, it rubs us the wrong way. We have two choices. Maybe three. We can get mad and react immediately; we can recognize the spirit that is trying to attack us, or we can recognize something within ourselves that causes us to feel a certain way because the person truly meant no harm by it. If it is a spirit attempting to attack us, confront it. We are not to be scared to confront situations if we're doing it in the right spirit, but we have to put on the full armor of our protection first.

Before we can fight the enemy, we have to take off our flesh and put on the WHOLE armor. In order to enter into spiritual warfare and be witnesses to others, we have to put prayer into our work. Put away the flesh and put on Christ in order to speak with boldness or with love and wisdom.

There are so many scriptures that point to your shield, your protection, and how we are to fight! Here are a few. If you would like the full material and Bible study PowerPoint for this section, please email me at marsbar9992002@gmail.com.

Revelation 11:8
1 Chronicles 12:33–38
Romans 13:14
Exodus 15:3
Genesis 3:1
Psalm 18:34
Psalm 3:3
Second Timothy 2:1–4

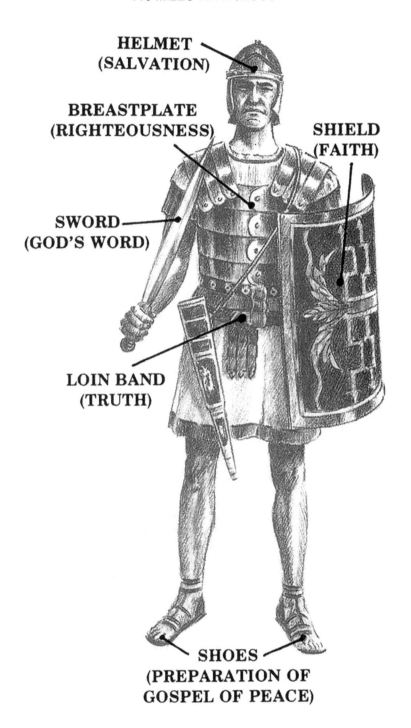

The Gates of Hell

After an AMAZING church service, during a time when the rest of my family was not serving God, I was at the altar praying for them. The Lord spoke to me loud and clear.

He said, "Go down to the pits of hell and get them!"

My response was, "How? They're so far gone. How?"

He said, "The Gates of hell shall not prevail. Put on your armor, take your angels with you, and GO GET THEM!"

I immediately envisioned myself walking down through the fire to the depths of the earth. I saw and felt two angels behind me. Protecting me from the flames and the enemy. I looked "him" straight in the eyes and screamed as loud as possible.

"THEY DON'T BELONG TO YOU. THEY BELONG TO HIM! RELEASE THEM NOW! IN THE NAME OF JESUS!"

I marched right back up with their souls in my hand and continued to speak in tongues as long as the Lord required me. When I came back into my flesh, I looked around, slightly embarrassed. I saw just a few people standing around in the sanctuary. The next morning, on a run with a friend, I told her about the experience at the altar. My friend's response was, "I know me and Melissa were there, and we had our arms stretched out behind you, praying with you." I instantly knew why I recognized the angels behind me that night. Those two powerful women of God were my angels. They were walking with me on my journey.

You are not alone when you are fighting a spiritual battle. You have angels by your side! Don't be afraid to command the enemy. Don't be afraid to fight spirits that your loved ones can't. Be prepared to fight when God tells you to! He will send others to fight with you!

You Are Not Alone!

How are you going to crush the enemy today? Be specific in your plan. Put on your full armor, take your angels with you, and defeat whatever GIANT is in your way!

___

Sour Grapes

Being a caretaker is hard! Lord, how do I care for her when she barely cared for me? Your word says, "Honor thy father and thy mother," but HOW? How do I do this without being bitter?

You need to be her caretaker, not her daughter. You learn how to forgive, truly forgive. Be compassionate, caring, and kind. You teach your boys how to love elderly parents.

You are a caretaker now for an example later.

It's hard. I'm not doing it right. I make mistakes every day. I am ashamed that it's this hard. I can't do it.

Oh, but daughter, you are doing it. Not perfectly, but you're doing it. You're doing the best you can right now. It will improve. It will get easier. You will learn, and you will show grace and mercy.

A very real conversation between God and me regarding my mother, who suddenly fell into dementia and into my life. We have always had a strained relationship. We have both tried to do our best to make it tolerable throughout my life. She did her best. I realize that. She could have, should have done more. But she did her best. Now being the only one available in my family, I do my best. Each day, I wake up and pray that the Lord gives me patience, love, and mercy so I can give it to her. I am doing my best right now.

I have learned how to forgive the past. The should have, could have beens. I have learned that honor doesn't mean to dote upon. Honor doesn't mean slave or doormat. Honor means respect, care, and show love like Christ. I do it for strangers, and I can do it for her. I am not her daughter anymore. I am her caretaker.

Bitterness has no place in God's vessels. Everyone has something from their childhood that could cause anger, bitterness, or unforgiveness. Pray that God takes care of it for you. Pray that God shows you how to forgive THEM for the purpose of healing YOU.

Whether your upbringing was full of laughter and joy or you don't know your parents, or if you're somewhere in between those two scenarios, what is something from your childhood that you need to forgive your parents of? Tell God how it hurts so he can heal it.

Hide-and-Seek

Driving along, praying, and loving the Lord today, right before New Year's Eve service. Foot washing, Communion, and a restart are about to take place tonight, so exciting!

GOD: Give it to me

ME: Well, good morning to you too.

GOD: Give it to me (like a master telling his dog to give him something that he shouldn't have in his mouth)

ME: What? I don't have anything. I just want to love on you today.

GOD: You might as well give it to me because I know you're hiding it.

ME: This? Oh, it's nothing. I'm working it out. It'll be gone by tomorrow. You know, New Year, new me.

GOD: Nope. Give it to me now. I want to crush it before you come to me with communion. Communion is for the cleansed, not the dirty. Don't drink my blood or eat my body in vain.

Drop it NOW!

ME: Well, she and then I feel like I. Do you see why I feel this way, you understand? You see why I'm feeling this way, right?!

GOD: Nope. Give it to me so I can fix it.

ME: Anger and shame flood me all at once, and I'm sorry, Lord, but how embarrassing it is to have to tell her how I've been feeling. I know it's not her fault.

GOD: Do it. Wash her feet. Apologize. It's good for YOU.

ME: Yes, Lord. Thank you for letting me see something I was trying to ignore.

Jealousy, bitterness, envy, and strife...lay it at his feet. Casting every weight of sin...

110 MILES WITH JESUS

What is something that you are holding onto that needs to be addressed with God or with another person?

Ewwww!

I have digestion issues. I get constipated. There, I said it. Everyone does it. We just do it differently. And if you know me and ever approach me to discuss my digestion issues, I will deny I ever knew you. The problem is, when I get stressed out, everything stays in. It brings me physical pain.

Debilitating pain. It creates pain in other areas of my body besides my intestines. However, when the stress is released, other things are released. I feel better and lighter—happier.

> And if they be bound in fetters,
> And be holden in cords of affliction;
> Then he sheweth them their work,
> And their transgressions that they have exceeded.
> He openeth also their ear to discipline,
> And commandeth that they return from iniquity.
> If they obey and serve him,
> They shall spend their days in prosperity,
> And their years in pleasures. (Job 36:8–11)

> Verily I say unto you, What things soever ye shall bind on earth shall be bound in heaven; and what things soever ye shall loose on earth shall be loosed in heaven. (Matthew 18:18)

According to the Oxford Dictionary, the definition of "affliction" is something that causes pain or suffering. Sometimes we do this to ourselves. Bind ourselves up and create havoc in our own system. Sometimes, it's the enemy that binds us. The problem is when we feel bound, it causes problems in other areas of our lives. Being bound causes problems in our marriage, in our relationships with our children, and in our relationships with others.

This is not how God wants us to live. He does not want us to feel bound. God's word is not contradictory. His word says he came to set the captive free. How can you be free if you are bound?

Let go. Give him everything so that you can be free. When you are lighter on your feet, the enemy can't trip you up.

Humble yourselves therefore under
the mighty hand of God, that he may
exalt you in due time: casting all your
care upon him; for he careth for you. (1 Peter 5:6–7)

What can you release to God to give you more? What is binding you? Freedom and less pain?

Time For a Test

On a history exam, a question was posed. I didn't know much about history before this course. I didn't care all that much about it during or after. I care about people. I care about how they are treated. My eyes perked up when I read the following question. No matter the score of the exam or even this one question, I am proud of my answer.

Love One Another

Q: What is a frequent result in societies, nations, organizations, and families where there is fear? Why is that? A: Ultimately, fear creates either panic, paralysis, or irrational thought. When a society or individual is fearful, the reasoning mechanism in their mind shifts to a fight-or-flight state of mind. This causes one to create unnecessary defense or attempt to escape. In the settlers' case, fear of not having enough resources caused unnecessary wars/battles and previous land owners to retreat and give up what was rightfully theirs. I believe that each preexisting inhabitant could have and did attempt to live in harmony with those who came to establish the same goals that were already here.

1 John 4:18 of the Holy Bible states, "There is no fear in love, but perfect love casteth out fear: because fear hath torment. He that feareth is not made perfect in love. We love him because he first loved us." When we choose to love our fellow man, we will have no reason to fear. When we have no fear, we are able to love our fellow man as well as our creator.

> Though I speak with the tongues of men and of angels, and have not charity, I am become as sounding brass, or a tinkling cymbal. (1 Corinthians 13:1, read the whole chapter)

How will you or do you show love to your fellow man?

It Is Finished?

After moving from Florida to Georgia, for so many Godly reasons, it would take another book to tell them all to you. Just know that God wanted us to be broken, healed, and restored to a deeper level during this time. We did not know anyone here, but I knew I had a calling. So we reached out to our community, we prayed, and we sought for somewhat of a life that we had in Florida. God didn't want that. He wanted something new.

I Wanted to Keep Deaf Ministry Alive!

I sought the Deaf community in the area. I sought a ministry that he put in me for a purpose. That seeking was unsuccessful. I found Deaf friends, but none that wanted to be involved in the ministry I was trying to keep alive. I asked a friend one day, maybe just stated it, but it was posed as "this ministry is dead." Her response was so beautiful, and I'm thankful that she sought wisdom to give to me.

"It's not dead, it's just dormant. God doesn't give you a gift just to take it away."

From that day on, I didn't push anything regarding that ministry but sought after new things from God. He gave them to me. He gave me Bible studies to teach, he gave me friendships in areas I would have never imagined, and he gave me depth to his word. Later, when I wasn't expecting it, I was called to interpret in other locations. I was invited to interpret online Sunday mornings for a church that needed help with deaf ministry. It did not conflict with my home church schedule, and it was a way for God to let me know that this ministry is NOT DEAD.

For the gifts and calling of God are without repentance. (Romans 11:29)

110 MILES WITH JESUS

What is something that God has called you to that you have not yet seen the fruit? Is it dead or just dormant?

Fruits of the Spirit

I took NINE weeks to teach a Bible study to a group of ladies about the fruits of the Spirit. We grew our trunks and our branches in order to produce fruit.

> *But the fruit of the Spirit is love, joy, peace, longsuffering, gentleness, goodness, faith, meekness, temperance: against such there is no law. (Galatians 5:22–23)*

And he shall be like a tree planted by the rivers of water, That bringeth forth his fruit in his season; His leaf also shall not wither; And whatsoever he doeth shall prosper. (**Psalm 1:3**)

Recap of the nine fruits.
- **Love:** Paul tells the Roman Church HOW MUCH God loved them (**Romans 8:37**)!
- **Joy:** When this world lets you down, where can you turn? To Jesus! He gives you the joy that your soul desires (**Psalm 16:11**)!
- **Peace:** The woman with the issue of blood. She had to press through so many people just to get to Jesus, but just KNOWING that if she could just touch a small part of him, she would be healed! OH, JUST TO TOUCH HIM! But once we do…what a blessing of peace we have (**Mark 5:25–35**)!
- **Long-suffering:** Jesus, Peter, and Paul were all LONG-SUFFERING for the sake of the gospel! Are we willing to do the same (**2 Peter 3:15**)?
- **Goodness:** The root word is good. Good can mean many things, including being valuable and desirable. We are desired by Satan for the sake of destruction, but more so, by Jesus for the sake of salvation (**Luke 22:31-32**)!

- **Faith:** Whenever your faith is short or not full, please read this chapter over and over. It will lift you up…if you can, you believe my testimonies and the things that God IS ABLE to do! Can you believe in God, whom you have not seen (**Hebrews 11:1–6**)?
- **Temperance:** In today's society, it's not common to stay away from things that "make you feel good," but the Bible speaks differently (**2 Corinthians 6:17**).
- **Gentleness: 2 Timothy 2:24–25**
- **Meekness:** We have to MAKE PEACE. It doesn't just happen; we have to make it happen. By the words we choose (or the ones we choose not to use), the tone of voice we use, and our actions. All this is done through wisdom. When God gives us the wisdom we need, we can be everything else, meek and gentle (Titus 3:1–2).

Even so, every good tree bringeth forth good fruit, but a corrupt tree bringeth forth evil fruit. A good tree cannot bring forth evil fruit, and neither can a corrupt tree bring forth good fruit. Every tree that bringeth not forth good fruit is hewn down and cast into the fire. Wherefore by their fruits, ye shall know them. Not everyone that saith unto me, Lord, Lord, shall enter into the kingdom of heaven; but he that doeth the will of my Father which is in heaven (**Matthew 7:17–21**).

MARLO COKER

Love

An intense feeling of deep affection, a great interest, and pleasure in something.

The Four Types of Love
Some Are Healthy, Some Are Not

- Eros: erotic, passionate love; this is what we're used to experiencing with our spouses and significant others—human love.
- Philia: love of friends and equals
- Storge: love of parents for children.
- Agape: love of mankind—God's love.

Since the very beginning of creation, God has wanted a relationship with mankind, from walking in the cool of the garden with Adam and Eve to the present day. He has done EVERYTHING to build a relationship with us.

> Nay, in all these things we are more than conquerors through him that loved us. For I am persuaded, that neither death, nor life, nor angels, nor principalities, nor powers, nor things present, nor things to come, nor height, nor depth, nor any other creature, shall be able to separate us from the love of God, which is in Christ Jesus our Lord. (Romans 8:37–39)

Now we get to the heart of God's agape love. He died on a cross for us. He was bloody, bruised, and buried for our sins. BUT he also rose again and created this whole new way to be in his presence. However, he also wants us to live in the newness of life. Sin no more, but when we do, because we are sinners by nature, we must ask for forgiveness and cleanse our hearts so we can continue walking in his love. Because God is not mocked (Galatians 6:7), we can't say we love God and then continue to hurt him! Essentially sending him to the cross over and over. God loves us unconditionally, yes, but why would you want to hurt somebody who loves you and you love them? God's love cannot be stopped, but we can stop ourselves from receiving that love.

I am living proof of how I once loved God but still hurt him, but I am also living proof that God loved me enough to stay by my side.

(Loving people is hard sometimes. Especially if you're trying to win souls and have been hurt in doing so, pray that you see them through God's eyes. I encourage you to read *For the Love of Dirt* by Denee Richardson.)

My testimony of HIS love for me is this…How can you show love to others?

110 MILES WITH JESUS

Joy

Joy can be a noun or verb.

Joy, as a noun, can be heaven! Hebrews 12:2 KJV says, "Looking unto Jesus the author and finisher of our faith; who for the joy that was set before him endured the cross, despising the shame, and is set down at the right hand of the throne of God."

As a verb, it is an emotion. The Oxford Dictionary describes joy as "a feeling of great pleasure and happiness."

More specifically, it is an INTRANSITIVE VERB, meaning an intransitive verb is a verb whose meaning does not include any particular object!

So when we talk about biblical joy, we know that it comes from the Lord! And only the Lord! It is a continual, forward-moving gladness of the heart that comes from knowing, experiencing, and trusting Jesus that we can't get from anywhere in this world!

It's very easy to look at people and say, "You make me so happy! You give me such joy!"

It's even easy to feel depressed when we don't see or talk to our favorite people, and it possibly causes us to lose our joy for a season. In fact, I'll give you a personal example of what happened recently. I was not hearing from my friends from Florida, and the enemy tried to use that against me.

"See, you are alone. Nobody cares about you...blah blah blah," You know what I did? I got into the word! Just like Jesus did when he went into the wilderness. In Matthew 4, Jesus continually used the very word HE created to destroy the words that the enemy tried to use to tempt him. I literally googled biblical words of affirmation and Bible studies that would help me create joy in my soul.

I found Psalm 16 and read it out loud! Look at verse 11, "Thou wilt shew me the path of life: in thy presence is fullness of joy; at thy right hand there is pleasure for evermore."

Immediately after reading this Psalm (and other scriptures), my tears dried up, and my joy was restored!

It's okay to respect and honor a person, but as long as we don't look to them as our savior or the one that satisfies us. Look at the story of Esther and how easy it would have been for the Jewish community to sing praises and worship Esther for taking the faithful steps to go before the king on behalf of her people. But the Jewish community knew better.

The Jews had light, and gladness, and joy, and honor. (Esther 8:16)

Joy comes from God, which brings contentment, and it's everlasting!

When you feel overwhelmed, frustrated, angry, or sad, what can you do to bring joy back into your soul?

Peace

What do you know about peace? What stories can you relate to in the Bible that talk about peace? Mary, Martha's sister, twice sits at Jesus's feet.

- With the Alabaster box pouring anointing oil (John 12:3–8)
    - There are times in the prayer room, I want to pour out everything I have, no matter the cost, no matter the rebuke or thoughts from others. I'm not there to care what they think, only that Jesus approves of my worship. I am at peace knowing I am giving everything that I have to the one who gave his life for me.
    - Other times in the prayer room, I just sit at the feet of Jesus listening to him speak to others and then speak to him. Like a little girl, knowing he's right by my side. He doesn't have to speak directly to me to know that he's close, I am at peace just feeling his presence.
- Woman at the well (John 4:5–42)
    - Have you ever just sat and talked to Jesus? Not because you want or need something, not because you're travailing for someone but just to have a conversation with him? It's done in peace! It's like having a cup of coffee with a friend where one conversation leads to another, and you're just in this mode of "I can sit here all day." Peace doesn't always mean quiet. It means to be still and calm.
- The adulteress (John 8:1–11)

Are you wondering how a screaming woman being dragged from her home and accused of adultery while an angry crowd looks on, ready to stone her, relates to peace? Look at the last few scriptures. Jesus is able to send away all of her accusers with the written word! Let him speak for you while you just sit and wait. That is peace.

Notice that in the end, she gets to be alone with Jesus. He just lets her talk and then sends her on her way, a forgiven and free woman!

- Jesus in the boat during the storm (Mark 4:35–39)
  - And the famous analogy, "Sometimes, Jesus calms us, and sometimes, he calms the storm." In this case, he calms the storm. Takes care of the situation while he stays calm and those around him are in such fear and anxiety. Let Jesus calm the storm that rages inside of you! Let him speak peace to your situation and calm you!
- The woman with the issue of blood (Mark 5:25–35)
  - This is the only account in the Bible whereby the touch of his garment was "virtue"/POWER noticeably gone from Jesus! This woman had such desperation and faith to get to him that he noticed her without even intentionally healing her!
  - This woman had to press through so many people! Have you ever had to do that? Press through so much just to get to Jesus but just KNOWING that if you could just touch a small part of him, your situation could be solved. We have to fight through our own thoughts, the things of this world, and the years of torment and pain JUST TO TOUCH HIM! But once we do, what a blessing of peace we have!

What kind of peace do you need from Jesus today? How can he calm you? What are you willing to do for the peace that you've read about today?

Gentleness and Meekness

Gentleness: Sensitivity of disposition and kindness of behavior, founded on strength and prompted by love
Meekness: Gentle, mild, humble, tender temperament

First, let me say this. We have to MAKE PEACE, and it doesn't just happen, we have to make it happen. By the words we choose (or the ones we choose not to use), the tone of voice we use, and our actions. All this is done through wisdom. When God gives us the wisdom we need, we can be everything else, meek and gentle.

> A soft answer turneth away wrath: But grievous words stir up anger. The tongue of the wise useth knowledge aright: But the mouth of fools poureth out foolishness. (**Proverbs 15:1–2**)

> Who is a wise man and endued with knowledge among you? Let him shew out of a good conversation his works with meekness of wisdom. But if ye have bitter envying and strife in your hearts, glory not, and lie not against the truth. This wisdom descendeth not from above but is earthly, sensual, devilish. For where envying and strife are there is confusion and every evil work. But the wisdom that is from above is first pure, then peaceable, gentle, and easy to be intreated, full of mercy and good fruits, without partiality, and without hypocrisy. And the fruit of righteousness is sown in peace of them that make peace. (**James 3:13–18**)

> A good example of what it means to have wisdom and how it correlates with meekness and

110 MILES WITH JESUS

gentleness is to look at Solomon, David's son. (**1 Kings 3:16–28**)

Solomon didn't get emotional or upset at the two women, and he used gentleness and wisdom to solve the problem.

And the servant of the Lord must not strive; but be gentle unto all men, apt to teach, patient, in meekness instructing those that oppose themselves; if God peradventure will give them repentance to the acknowledging of the truth. (**2 Timothy 2:24–25**)

Where can you show gentleness and meekness? What can you do to turn away wrath?

Long-suffering

Ye have heard that it hath been said, Thou shalt love thy neighbor,
and hate thine enemy. But I say unto you, Love your enemies,
bless them that curse you, do good to them that hate you, and
pray for them which despitefully use you, and persecute you;
—Matthew 5:43–44

Patience in the trial that someone else is causing!

King David, before he was king. Read 1 Samuel this week.

Peter and Paul wrote the books of the New Testament. Most of
those books were letters to the churches or other apostles that they
were witnesses to for the gospel's sake, and most of those letters were
to correct errors that the saints had made. Peter and Paul were both
LONG-SUFFERING for the sake of the gospel!

For what glory is it, if, when ye be buffeted
for your faults, ye shall take it patiently? But
if, when ye do well, and suffer for it, ye take it
patiently, this is acceptable with God.

For even hereunto were ye called: because
Christ also suffered for us, leaving us an example,
that ye should follow his steps. (Peter 2:20–21)

They taught us how to love, even when we're not loved.

They taught us how to be soul-winners, even when it's hard and
there seems to be no reward. Out of all of the people that the disciples witnessed to, there were so many more that denied the gospel,
wanted to kill the apostles and refused Jesus. It's not our job to "win"
them to Christ.

It's our job to proclaim His name and then let them make the decision (**Acts 5:17, 9:23**).

> He that believeth and is baptized shall be saved; but he that believeth not shall be damned. And he said unto them, Go ye into all the world, and preach the gospel to every creature. (Mark 16:15–16)

Don't give up hope. Don't feel like you are not worthy or not effective. Even when they "persecute you," keep on loving them, loving God, trusting Him and doing what you know is right! The word and the Lord will fight your battles for you!

> And let us not be weary in well doing: for in due season we shall reap, if we faint not. Be not deceived; God is not mocked: for whatsoever a man soweth, that shall he also reap. (Galatians 6:7, 9)

Who is causing your suffering?

What are you suffering from?

110 MILES WITH JESUS

How can you combat it?

What do you feel you are doing right?

Why Am I Like This?

Recently, the enemy tried to highlight what could've been classified as a "social faux pas" because sometimes I can be too talkative or too loud or too _____. Reflecting on the incident, I looked up and asked, "Why am I like this, God?" the Lord immediately spoke to my soul and replied, "Because I made you that way!" I, of course, became an instant hot mess and thought about that statement, and this is what came about.

The world needs YOU. GOD needs YOU.

- The loud ones (to be bold)
- The quiet ones (to soften blows)
- The early risers (to pray before the daybreaks)
- The night owls (to pray light into the dark)
- The movers and shakers (to get things done)
- The rooted and grounded (to be the pillars)
- The visionaries (to help the Lord to do the impossible)
- The realists (to keep things in line)

Whoever, whatever God made you. Whatever gifts he gave you, USE THEM to the best of your ability and watch God give the increase!

> Ye have not chosen me, but I have chosen you, and ordained you, that ye should go and bring forth fruit, and that your fruit should remain: that whatsoever ye shall ask of the Father in my name, he may give it to you. (John 15:16 KJV)

List three characteristics that you claim as negative.

How can you change those characteristics into something that God can use for his purpose?

Goodness

Root word from etymonline.com, **good (adj.)**, "excellent, fine, valuable, desirable, favorable, beneficial; full, entire, complete;" "beneficial, effective; righteous, pious."

> And the Lord said, Simon, Simon, behold, Satan hath desired to have you, that he may sift you as wheat: but I have prayed for thee, that thy faith fail not: and when thou art converted, strengthen thy brethren. (Luke 22:31–32)

Because you are valuable to the kingdom, the enemy WILL attempt to steal you. He will attempt to isolate you, cause you to stray. Don't fall for it. Don't believe the lies that the enemy tells you that you are not valuable.

During the seven days of creation, after each day, God said, "It is Good." He made you. When he breathed breath into you, he finished his work in you. His work is good!

"You are important to the body of Christ! You are valuable to the kingdom!"

110 MILES WITH JESUS

He hath made everything beautiful in his time: also he hath set the world in their heart, so that no man can find out the work that God maketh from the beginning to the end. (Ecclesiastes 3:11)

What lies has the enemy told you recently?

_____

_____

_____

_____

_____

_____

_____

_____

_____

_____

Where do you see your value in the kingdom of God?

_____

_____

_____

_____

_____

_____

_____

_____

_____

_____

_____

_____

_____

_____

Church Hurt

It's real. It's painful. It's scarring. It shouldn't happen. But it does. I'm sure we've all experienced our fair share of being hurt by people who are supposed to love us like Christ. We have choices. We can get angry and lash back at those same people. We can lash out at others who have no idea why we're angry. We can also choose to realize that holding on to hurtful moments (because that's all they are, are moments) only causes angst in ourselves.

God doesn't want us to hold on to bitterness. Just like there are fruits of the Spirit, there are works of the flesh (Galatians 5:19). There are those who will attempt to cause division.

What do you do? First, you remember that you are not wrestling against flesh and blood but spirits of iniquity. Then you put on a smile, take all your concerns to God, and let him take care of it. I know it's easier said than done. I've been there. My whole family has been there.

I'll tell you the same thing that God gave me the wisdom to tell them.

We don't go to church for people.

They will fail us EVERY time. I have failed others. I can't say that I don't have blood on my hands. I pray that if I did hurt someone, they have learned that I am human, and they forgive me. I have repented for the actions and words that I know have hurt others.

We are not a perfect people. The church is not perfect.
Yet, God is!

We go to church to worship God. We go to show love to those that have never felt love from this world. You can break the cycle of hurt. You can help mend the scars someone else created. I have learned that there is so much healing in forgiveness of others and myself.

> But if ye bite and devour one another, take heed that ye be not consumed one of another. (Galatians 5:15)

> Not forsaking the assembling of ourselves together, as the manner of some is; but exhorting one another: and so much the more, as ye see the day approaching. (Hebrews 10:25)

Don't allow someone else to consume you. Allow God to consume your hurt.

What scars do you need to be healed? Can you be brave enough to hold your head high and smile at those that have hurt you? Can you truly forgive them?

Pay Attention

GOD: He's going to leave.

ME: What? Who? Where?

GOD: He's going to sneak out the back door when you're not expecting it.

ME: What? Who?

GOD: Watch him. Love him anyway. He'll come back.

ME: You're not making...oh...wait. No! DON'T LET HIM GO!

God: He's deciding for himself. Watch him. Love him. He'll come back.

That was over ten years ago. He's still not back.

Somewhere in my homeschooling, housewife/late-night server days, I got frustrated. Frustrated over not having enough money and frustrated over not getting any time for myself.

Frustrated over not using a degree that I had worked extremely hard for. I resented being "just" a stay-at-home wife/mother. Without talking to God, I went to work one day, told the restaurant manager that I was giving my two weeks' notice, and accepted an office job. I felt accomplished and successful—proud.

Until, approximately a month later, money still wasn't enough. The boys were fighting over screen time. Hubby and I were fighting over household chores. Older son resented the younger son because he had to be the babysitter. He resented me because he had to pick up some of the household chores. Hubby resented me for going back to work, and I resented going back to work. I was stubborn. I have a good work ethic. I DON'T QUIT ANYTHING.

My family suffered, and I let them. I watched it all happen before my eyes without realizing what was happening. And then...

There he went right out the door.

Eighteen, argumentative and sneaky. He snuck around. He lied. I didn't watch him. I got angry too many times. I pushed him away. I didn't love him like I should have.

I carried that guilt for a long time.

God warned me, but I didn't pay attention. I saw the signs, but I didn't pay attention. Things creeped in and out of my house, but I didn't pay attention.

I have learned to forgive myself. Love him for who he is now. He has learned to forgive me and love me despite who I was and who I am now. We have a good relationship now, but he has still walked away from God. I am holding on to the last promise. I am waiting.

Parents pay attention to the warning signs. When they make mistakes, don't push them away or be angry. Talk them through their feelings about WHY they are doing what they're doing. Pay attention to their behaviors, their friends, coworkers, their words, and their prayer life. Pay attention to God's voice and his warnings.

Pay attention.

How can you be more watchful in your family home? What do you notice that is off? How can you correct it?

I'm So Mad Today, God!

You promised me! You told me that this truth is for me and my house and my children and their children and ALL THOSE that are afar off. YOU PROMISED!

I saw it come to pass, but then I saw it diminish. They were here. All of them, my husband, the boys. They were right here.

And...

Now...

They're...

NOT!

I tried to follow your Word. I tried to be obedient. I tried to be a good example. One left and now the other, he's mad that the first one left and you won't answer his prayers. Now my head got cut off. He's offended. Blaming people that the boys left.

I'M MAD TOO! WHY AREN'T YOU SAVING THEM?

GOD: Are you done?

ME: NO! GO GET THEM! BRING THEM BACK!

GOD: I can't. But you're here. Come here. Let me hold you while you cry.

ME: No! I'm mad at you. BRING THEM BACK!

GOD: I can't. It's not in my will to see any perish. But it's also not in my will to override their will. I will send others to tell them how much you're hurting. I will send others to draw them back in. Trust me. Trust my plans.

ME: I do trust you, but I'm mad.

GOD: I know. Come here.

ME: (First a side hug, then a bear hug, and then sitting on his lap as he rocks me while I cry.) Protect them. Don't let them be harmed before you have a chance to save them.

GOD: **I love them more than you do. I died for them.**

ME: Thank you.

Grief is real, and It's not just for those that have physically passed. It can be for those that spiritually died. It can be for things and dreams and pets too.

If you need help dealing with your grief, I encourage you to read *Paws to Remember: A Journal Through Grief, Loss, and Recovery* by Teresa Billingsley.

MARLO COKER

What are you expecting from God today?

If you're mad, tell him. If you need a miracle, tell him. He already knows; don't hide away your pain. Let him hold you in order to heal you.

Shed your tears here. And then let God wipe them away.

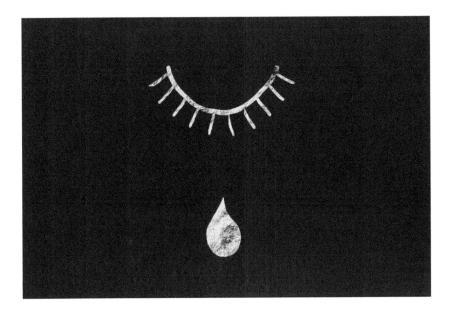

Sinews

Thus saith the Lord GOD unto these bones; Behold, I will cause breath to enter into you, and ye shall live: and I will lay SINEWS upon you, and will bring up flesh upon you, and cover you with skin, and put breath in you, and ye shall live; and ye shall know that I am the LORD.

—Ezekiel 37:5–6

Sinew: A piece of tough, fibrous tissue that unifies muscle to bone or bone to bone.

We are the body of Christ. We are many members but one body. We drink from one Spirit. When God puts all the pieces together, we live! You may be tough like muscles. You may be malleable, like soft skin. You may be dry and broken like the bones Ezekiel saw in the valley. Whatever part of the body you are, you cannot live without the sinews. The sinews cause blood flow! You must live in the body and allow his breath to enter into you. No matter how dry you are, hear the word of the Lord and allow it to prophesy to you! Let the body heal all of the broken parts, and let the blood flow freely!

Prophecy: A message from the Lord that WILL happen in the future.

The funny thing about a prophecy is that there is no exact timing of its completion. It could be one hour, one day, ten years, OR MORE. Ezekiel 37 is a good example of a promise that WILL come to pass, but not in the prophet's lifetime. It could even serve as an example of the metaphorical vs. literal meaning of a prophecy.

Hold on to the promises that God has given you. Just understand that it may not be when you want it or the way that you think it will happen. Continue trusting. Continue believing that all the working parts of the body WILL come together, in his timing, in his way.

110 MILES WITH JESUS

My prayers have been as simple as "Lord, I know you gave me this promise. I trust your timing. If it is in your will, I would like to see it come to pass. If not, I will be thankful that it happens after my time here on earth. Thank you for your promises."

What has been promised to you that you have yet to see come to pass?

_____

_____

_____

_____

_____

_____

_____

_____

_____

_____

What prayer will you pray that lets the Lord know that you still trust him?

_____

_____

_____

_____

_____

_____

_____

_____

_____

_____

_____

_____

_____

Which Way?

There I was, minding my own business while one of the littles that I was babysitting was napping.

"*Text Sister Denee and ask if you can go to South Korea with her.*"

"Cool! I'm on it!"

The response via text was not what I expected. My heart sank. I was confused.

> year. But you CAN go with me
> to Thailand
>
> 5:01 PM

I was sure that there was a miscommunication between the Lord and Sister Denee somewhere. Somehow, wires got crossed. Nope, it's another lesson! Through the weeks leading up to just DECIDING IF I WAS GOING TO BE OBEDIENT, there were many other things that were taking place. I can not to this day tell you how or why they were all connected. The only thing I can tell you is that the Lord wanted me to be obedient. I fully believe he was testing to see.

"*Is she going to pass my test of faith and obedience?*"

I did! I obeyed! I passed!

Through all of the doubt, grumbling, and unsurety, I passed!

And the whole time, God was just waiting in anticipation (not really, because nothing takes him by surprise) to open up the heavens and pour out his blessings! The blessings that were received and the once-in-a-lifetime experiences will not fit on this page. I am so thankful that I obeyed. I pray that out of all of the blessings received, there were others who received miracles as well. Nothing ever made the papers, but I know there was a purpose in the calling.

EVER PRAYING. EVER STRIVING. EVER EVOLVING.

I'm never surprised by God's blessings, only His (perfect) timing)!

*Almost a year ago, God prompted me to REALLY pay attention and take control of our finances (in hindsight, to do His will!)

*Through the process of freeing up our finances and my time, He called me to be a help to an unsuspecting leader, called me to Thailand AND prompted me to try my ASL skills in a new way...

*A little less than month ago, I came back home from Thailand and.THAT day was able to minister to a family in need

*3 weeks ago, I was asked to come to a meeting. At the same time, we were house hunting or deciding on if we should build

*2 weeks ago, my pastor preached on not letting opportunities pass you by

*Last week, ON THE SAME EXACT DAY I accepted the new challenge/opportunity/job/God's assignment...the offer that we put on a house (3 weeks ago) was accepted!

We will be closing on our house soon, fixing it up and hoping to move in by January with very little debt (only what we need to fix it up)!

I start my new job as a full time interpreter Dec 2nd. This week I'm in training. Just in time for me to be off of work for the holidays so I can help renovate our house. I'll be starting a new schedule and home life in January!

While I'm so sad to see my babies leave this Friday, "we know that in all things God works for the good of those who love him, who[a] have been called according to his purpose." Romans 8:28

"But seek ye first the kingdom of God, and his righteousness; and all these things shall be added unto you." Matthew 6:33

What crazy thing has the Lord asked you to do? When you obeyed, was it the reaction, response, or outcome that you expected?

_____
_____
_____
_____
_____
_____
_____
_____
_____
_____
_____
_____
_____
_____

Faith

It's powerful. It's the first step to ANYTHING that we want to experience.

> God, I thank you for the word that is about to go forth. I thank you for the burden that you have given all who teach Bible studies and all who come to hear and be taught your Word. I pray that each one who hears and reads the word will open their hearts and their minds to receive exactly what you have for them and that you do the work to give them the faith and the trust that they need to get them through whatever they are facing in their lives. Let your word be a light unto their path and hope for their future. In Jesus' precious name. AMEN.

Faith means to have complete trust or confidence in someone or something—TRUST. Faith and trust go hand in hand. But how do we get it? Do we naturally have faith in something? Anything, whether it be God, a person, or a certain religion? How do we establish faith? We do it through experience. Think about a baby. When a baby is born, it automatically trusts that its needs will be met.

Humanity, naturally has the power to either meet those needs or not. The baby, in response, learns how to react based on which way it goes. When an infant cries, it knows that its needs will be met. If its needs aren't met, they naturally learn to soothe themselves. If they go too long without those needs, they die. If they survive, as the infant goes through life and starts growing and experiencing the world, they learn what to trust and what not to trust. They learn where to put their faith. Each experience as life progresses teaches that. When they don't know something, they look to others for social cues and experiences.

Now let's take all that natural knowledge and apply it to the spiritual context. Some of us grow up knowing who God is because we were brought to church or prayer meetings our whole lives. We have been fed the proper spiritual nutrition and have learned to trust and have faith based on experiences. Some of us have not. Some of us have been spiritually dying since we were born but still trying to figure out how to be fed. Some have died. Some have merely survived. Some have watched others survive and have taken spiritual cues on how to do so. But at some point, we have heard about God. That's why we're here. We've heard about him, and we've seen others serve him, so we've tried to demonstrate what's been modeled, received nourishment from it, and even learned something for ourselves from it.

Romans 10:17 says, "Faith comes by hearing and hearing by the word of God."

Read Hebrews 11. Yes, all of it.

(Email me at marsbar9992002@gmail.com if you want the whole seven-page study on faith.)

Temperance

Have self-control. This could be in the realm of many things: your emotions, temptations, or thoughts.

2 Peter 1:1–11, This part of the chapter relates temperance to faith, patience, godliness, and virtue and then encompasses all of it with salvation. So basically, without knowing who Jesus is, what he has done for us, and what he can do for us, we can't have temperance, and without temperance, we can't have salvation.

WE HAVE TO HAVE SELF-CONTROL in order to be saved! We have to push aside all of the temptations of this world. All the emotional diarrhea that we want to push onto others has to be contained and given to Jesus!

> Choosing rather to suffer affliction with the
> people of God, than to enjoy the pleasures of sin
> for a season. (Hebrews 11:25)

When Googling "temperance," one definition means to be sober. Biblically, there are two or three scriptures that use the word, but most of the scriptures point to drunkenness.

Have you ever noticed that people usually use alcohol and other substances in order to unleash their inhibitions? Alcohol doesn't just cause you to be drunk, it causes you to let go of your self-control. It causes you to do things you wouldn't normally do if you were sober. It hurts relationships. It brings out emotions that you've been suppressing.

In today's society, it's not common to stay away from things that "make you feel good," we're all about "you do you, boo!" but the Bible speaks differently.

2 Corinthians 6:17 says, "Wherefore come out from among them, and be ye separate, saith the Lord and touch not the unclean thing; and I will receive you."

Whenever we see "wherefore" in the Bible, we have to look above that particular scripture to find the reason it's there for, starting in verse 14 (read to 17). Verse 16 says that the temple of God cannot have idols in it. An idol can be anything that we value more than God himself. We have the fruits of the Spirit because HE lives in us. But he cannot live in us if we allow idols or unclean things to live in us or in our minds.

Ephesians 4:27 says, "Neither give place to the devil." Meaning that if you allow just a little bit of something that you're tempted by, you're allowing the enemy to come in to create more temptation.

Read Psalm 19 and focus on 19:13.

What is something or multiple things that you are willfully allowing in your life?

What area of your life can you use more self-control?

Rejoice with Me!

God! You found him! You found my head! I thought it was cut off. I thought I would never see it again, but you found it! You found his heart! You softened it! Thank you, Lord!

I know we had to give up our home. We had to go to unfamiliar territory. But we found him! You found him!

"Yes, now be gentle. He's still wounded. He needs to rest. He needs to heal."

But...I want to squeeze him so hard! I want to tell him all of the ways I went looking for him. I want to tell him how he hurt me while he was gone. I want to open up to him, and I want him to open up to me and tell me why he was gone for so long. I want to tell him all of the things and know all the things, and I want him to tell me all of the things I want.

Stop! Take a breath! Let me heal him. Don't suffocate him before I can put my breath back in him. He will open up when he's ready. In the meantime, just rejoice that he's back! Rest with him.

Thank You! Hallelujah! Thank you! Hallelujah! Thank you!

> And when she hath found it, she calleth her friends and her neighbors together, saying, Rejoice with me; for I have found the piece which I had lost.
>
> Luke 15:9

For clarity purposes, my husband did not ever physically leave our home or me, but he did leave the church and walked away from God's truth in his life. There were times that I felt that he had left me emotionally. I was very grateful when God softened his heart to bring him back to me emotionally and spiritually.

Have you rejoiced with your friends for their loved ones coming home?

110 MILES WITH JESUS

_____

Have you become bitter because their family came home and yours hasn't?

_____

Pray that God allows you to rejoice with those that rejoice. YOURS ARE COMING BACK TOO! IN THE MEANTIME...
Who will you rejoice with for their miracle?

_____

Create your prayer list here.

_____

Graduation-Gradually Gravitating Upward

Graduating is a peculiar thing. It starts at Pre-K; parents are excited for their little ones to elevate from one milestone to another. Then it's kindergarten to elementary, elementary to middle, middle to high, high school to bachelor's (if one so desires), potentially bachelor's to master's, and then finally, there's an end to it all with a doctorate. I used to have the mindset that all the ceremonies up until high school were arbitrary.

Why celebrate such a low level of Pre-K knowing that they will be walking off a platform just to walk right back into a classroom?

Why not?

Why not celebrate each milestone of accomplishment?

Why not celebrate each step toward a higher degree of success?

Scripture tells us that every step of faith brings us closer to repentance, salvation, and relationship with him!

Celebrate the daily successes. Celebrate the big days and the little days. Celebrate that you're breathing. Right Now!

This is the day which the LORD hath made;
We will rejoice and be glad in it. (Psalm 118:24)

No Matter where you are in your walk of faith, celebrate where you are. And then Strive to go higher.

110 MILES WITH JESUS

What are some milestones you've reached in God recently?

Now how can you go further?

Judges

"Don't judge me, I am who I am" (the world).
"Don't judge others unless you want to be judged" (Jesus).
"Judge yourself so Jesus doesn't have to judge us harshly" (Paul).

Just before another new transition, a move into uncharted territory, Jesus said, "Study Judges." I took the morning to read the whole book of Judges, made some notes and highlights and was pretty proud of myself.

God: Good, now STUDY IT!
ME: "I DID!" (I was in a mood that day.)
God: No! (I put him in a mood.) You read it, now STUDY IT!

I took the next week to study WHY God set up judges during that time period. I studied the characteristics of each one. I figured out how I related to them and I figured out how they could be an example to me for the next season I was about to walk into. I STUDIED JUDGES. God was satisfied. That was the easy part. Now I needed to apply the knowledge. That is the hard part.

I'm still learning from Deborah (three years later). I feel I have a good handle on Gideon's spirit.

I've been delivered from a Samson spirit. (In the end, he knew how to connect with God and helped save a nation.)

Read about the judges on your own and email me if you would like more notes, but I do want to point out some key facts within the book:

- God shows mercy and favor again and again, just trying to get his people to take the right path!
- Take notice of the TWELVE judges, TWELVE tribes of Judah, and TWELVE apostles: Twelve is one of God's favorite numbers that represents completeness.

- It just takes ONE person to be obedient and used and fulfill God's plan
- God rules over us but sends others to shift us back into his presence.

So it is not people that are suppose to judge other people, but we are to judge situations and actions of others when they are not right. We have to be sure that we are doing it with the right motive. Are we judging others in order to tear them down and build ourselves up? Or are we doing it to be a help to their soul? Take on the characteristics of Jesus, his disciples, and his judges in order to reach those who don't realize how much they need help.

> But let a man examine himself, and so let him eat of that bread, and drink of that cup. For he that eateth and drinketh unworthily, eateth and drinketh damnation to himself, not discerning the Lord's body. For this cause, many are weak and sickly among you, and many sleep. For if we would judge ourselves, we should not be judged. But when we are judged, we are chastened of the Lord, that we should not be condemned with the world. Wherefore, my brethren, when ye come together to eat, tarry one for another. And if any man hunger, let him eat at home; that ye come not together unto condemnation. And the rest will I set in order when I come. (1 Corinthians 11:28–32)

> Judge not, that ye be not judged. For with what judgment ye judge, ye shall be judged: and with what measure ye mete, it shall be measured to you again. (Matthew 7:1–6)

Are you judging to be a help or a hindrance?

What characteristics from each of the judges do you see in yourself?

Porters

I'm driving along, listening to the assigned (and boring to me) chapters for the day. 1 Chronicles. Lineage. Heritage. History that has already been recorded in previous books. Really, as you can tell, I was doing more complaining than listening. And then…

"In four quarters were the porters."

ME: Hehe, that rhymed. In a singsong, nursery-rhyme tone, "In four quarters were porters, in four quarters were porters" (forgetting that the rest of the chapter was still playing).

GOD: You're complaining about my word. You're ignoring my word. You're making fun of my word. Go STUDY IT!

(If you have read other topics, have you noticed a homework theme when I'm in trouble? EEK!)

Porter Definition
1. Gate/Doorkeeper
2. One that waits at the door to receive messages
3. A person who carries/conveys burdens for hire
4. Wise servant of God
5. Soldiers of the Lord and guards of the house

Chief Porter
- AKA Maimonides
- Walked around the city, passing other gatekeepers, would say, "Peace be unto you."
- If a porter was asleep as the chief passed by, he would strike him and had the right to set his clothes on FIRE!

We need to be gatekeepers of the word, righteousness, and our brothers and sisters in Christ. We need to get to a point where my fire is infectious enough to set others on fire. If you're sleeping, I want to be able to give you a Holy Ghost slap, and you not get offended, but you WAKE UP! AND I want you to be able to do it to me!

Look at all of these scriptures pertaining to our responsibility. "God caused Adam to sleep and then created a helpmeet for him" (Genesis 2:21–23).

- Confess our faults for the purpose of healing (James 5:14–19).
- We can be each other's helpmeet (Galatians 6:1–2).
- When they "laid hands on them" / struck them, they received the Holy Ghost (Acts 8:17).
- Provoke one another to good works (Hebrews 10:24–25).

Do you take your responsibility as a gatekeeper seriously?

_____

_____

_____

_____

_____

_____

Are you actively watching and waking your brothers/sisters up?

_____

_____

_____

_____

_____

Are you dispensing peace as you guard the gates?

_____

_____

_____

_____

_____

You've Been Subitized

To perceive the number of items in a group without counting them.
—Oxford Dictionary

I learned this word while working in a first-grade classroom. The kids are expected, and they do, to know a specific number of dots on a die or on a card without counting them. It's pretty impressive!

So there I am, driving in my car, pulling the tangles out of my hair, smoothing it out to be "perfect." A clump of hair comes out, as it often does when I brush or finger out the tangles. I throw the clump out the window and immediately ask.

"Do you still know the number of hairs on my head? What if I pull out more? Do you have to count them all over again?"

His reply was very simple, almost in an amused tone, and a little wink at the end.

> But the very hairs of your head are all numbered. Fear ye not therefore, ye are of more value than many sparrows. (Matthew 10:30–31)

He knows you. He knows the hairs on your head just as much as he knows your heart, even when it changes. He doesn't keep count of your wrongs or your rights. He only needs to look at you and know how valuable you are.

110 MILES WITH JESUS

What is a silly question you've asked God recently?

How did he respond?

What is a scripture that God has let you know how valuable you are to him?

What are your notes for that particular scripture?

I Am for You, Not against You...

One night, during a not-so-easy conversation with hubby, we were getting agitated with each other over a situation that we both wanted the best of but had different opinions about how to resolve it.

As we were disagreeing, I realized and said out loud, "We both want the same thing. We just have different avenues to get to the same goal." and then God showed up. In our living room, he showed up and spoke. The next words out of my mouth were,

"Babe, you are my husband. I love you. I am for you, not against you."

His response was "yeah, but…" so I said it again.

"Babe, you are my husband. I love you. I am for you, not against you and I need you to say it back to me."

He did and then we were able to finish our conversation that was previously an argument. We did it with respect, hearing each other's perspectives, and came to a rational, agreeable solution.

After that night, there were other times when we would just be together, not in any conversation or disagreement, and I would look at him and say, "Hey, babe…," and he would respond with, "I love you. You are my wife, and I am for you, not against you."

There are other times when I'm stressed and frustrated, and he will now say it to me first.

I love that it's our way of letting the other know that we are on each other's side and we are one flesh. The enemy is NOT going to separate this couple!

110 MILES WITH JESUS

What is something you can do to relieve tension in discussions with your spouse or communication partner?

_____

_____

_____

_____

_____

_____

_____

How do you think they will respond?

_____

_____

_____

_____

_____

_____

_____

What will you do to help them understand what kind of response you need from them?

_____

_____

_____

_____

_____

_____

And if one prevail against him, two shall withstand him; and a threefold cord is not quickly broken. (Ecclesiastes 4:12)

Lazarus, Come Forth!

> And when he thus had spoken, he cried
> with a loud voice, Lazarus, come forth. And he
> that was dead came forth, bound hand and foot
> with graveclothes: and his face was bound about
> with a napkin. Jesus saith unto them, Loose him,
> and let him go.
>
> —John 11:43–44

Right before this, Mary and Martha are berating Jesus because he didn't come in time. He wasn't there when his friend was dying. He let Lazarus die. Jesus knew he was sick, and he didn't come. But he did! He came at the right time in order to perform one of many miracles!

Take notice that Martha asked Jesus to help her, yet was mad at him as he instructed her to be involved in the miracle about to take place. Nevertheless, he calls Lazarus out of the grave but tells "them" to loose him and let him go.

Jesus calls them out, and we unwrap the bondage of the world. We have the power to help them forget their past mistakes. We are not to remind them of their addictions, mistakes, or faults. We are supposed to help them from their bondages and then encourage them to run from the grave!

Just a few chapters later, we read Jesus tell Thomas and Phillip.

> Verily, verily, I say unto you, He that belie-
> veth on me, the works that I do shall he also do;
> and greater works than these shall he do; because
> I go unto my Father. (John 14:12)

Again, this is after both men are doubting who Jesus is and his true power. He tells them that if they believe him, if they do what I ask of them with true faith, they will be involved in the miracles. Not only do they get to be involved, they are able to do more than what they had already seen. How cool is that? God wants us to be involved

110 MILES WITH JESUS

in his work! He understands that we will not always fully understand the magnitude of the miracle, but he wants us to participate with him! Wow!

There will always be doubters and scoffers in a miracle not yet seen. What if we stick around to not only witness it but to have the opportunity to have our hands in it! When we do, we get to go on amazing adventures with him! We get to write books about our experiences! We get to tell others our testimonies that may build their faith and help save their soul!

> And they overcame him by the blood of
> the Lamb, and by the word of their testimony;
> and they loved not their lives unto the death.
> (Revelation 12:11)

> Come Forth!

And you will have opportunities to watch miracles take place right before your eyes! So much so that it becomes commonplace!

How would you like to participate in a miracle (or several)?

_____

_____

_____

_____

_____

_____

What have you already seen so far that has become the norm?

_____

_____

_____

_____

_____

_____

Down to Your Level

Feeling a little down today? Feeling like you are not in the right headspace to talk to Jesus today? Feeling like somebody dragged you out of your house, through the mud, and ready to cast stones at you? Feeling like an utter failure?

I have great news. Jesus still loves you. He still wants to talk to you. So much that he will even stoop down to your level just to have a private conversation with you.

Here's the thing: when he does, when he kneels to you, you only have one option after that. When he stands, you have to lift your head and stand too. You have to look around and realize that all your accusers have left because Jesus spoke on your behalf.

Jesus will meet you where you are, but he does it so that he can elevate you up to his level. He does not want you to stay in the same condition he found you. In fact, he won't even let your enemies or negative influences stay around you after he's brought you up. He'll speak so profoundly on your behalf that he'll cause them all to drop their stones and walk away. You will have no adversaries.

Let Jesus come to you today. While others are running your name through the mud, you get to be alone with Jesus while he elevates you! How cool is that?

John 8:3–11 is a beautiful testimony of how much Jesus truly wants to forgive us and how much he wants us to forgive ourselves.

110 MILES WITH JESUS

What is something that others try to make you feel guilty of? Even if you know you made a mistake, you need Jesus to relieve your guilt.

Hyperboles

Did you know that most of the Bible was not to be taken literally? Especially the new testament. Don't close the page now. Just think about it. Most of Matthew is full of Jesus and parables. Did a farmer truly go out and sow seed? I'm sure he did. Are Jesus's instructions for us to go out into the literal field and throw seeds on the ground and wait for souls to pop out?

ABSOLUTELY NOT!
(that would be pretty cool or scary, depending on who you are)

What about going into the ocean and 'casting' our cares on him? How would that even be possible? Rent a boat, get a fishing pole, attach your notepad to it with all your concerns and launch it out as far as possible to see if it reaches heaven.

ABSURDITY!

So get this: everything we say and do is in his name, right? Then why does he say to be baptized in THE NAME OF *the Father,' the Son, and the Holy Ghost?*

Wouldn't he want us to be baptized IN HIS NAME? What is his name anyway? Well, Isaiah 9:6–7 tells us that "his name shall be called Wonderful, Counsellor, the mighty God, the everlasting Father, the Prince of Peace."

You're shouting at this page and saying,

THAT'S NOT HIS NAME!
YOU ARE CORRECT! (That's me shouting back)

Those are all characteristics of who he is! Just like father, son, and holy ghost are also titles/characteristics.

So you're asking yourself, but you're smart enough to already know the answer. "What does she think his name is?" "How is she going to tell me I should be baptized?" (Yes, I can read your mind. Not really, but he can.)

(Now that you've read it. Go DO IT!)

Shibboleth

Go ahead! Say it! Say it five times, fast!

Ooooh, aren't you in a silly mood today, Lord? You know I can't pronounce those hard words!

> *It's not that you can't pronounce them, it's that you don't try. And you certainly don't attempt to understand the importance of the big words.*

Oh, this is a lesson. Okay. What am I learning today?

> Study the word. DUH!
> (I told you, he was in a silly mood)

Shibboleth translates to flood. It was used as a password of sorts in order to cross over the "ditch." Without the correct pronunciation of this word, the Ephraimites (and others) could not cross over. In fact, they were killed.

Why is that the chosen word? Well, you need to know the name of living waters in order to overcome the ditch. It's the word that saves lives and brings them to the other side!

> But whosoever drinketh of the water that I shall give him shall never thirst; but the water that I shall give him shall be in him a well of water springing up into everlasting life. (John 4:14)

(Read verses 5–16 for full context)

Without the pronunciation of THE NAME, you cannot cross over. There's only ONE SAVING NAME!

> Then said they unto him, Say now Shibboleth: and he said Sibboleth: for he could

110 MILES WITH JESUS

> not frame to pronounce it right. Then they took him and slew him at the passages of Jordan: and there fell at that time of the Ephraimites forty and two thousand. (Judges 12:6)

I have made it a point that when I come across a word that I'm unfamiliar with, I take the time to study it. It has helped with my understanding of how each word is important and the meaning is always deeper than I expected. I still stumble over pronunciations, though.

What words in the Bible have you glossed over because you couldn't pronounce them?

_____

_____

_____

_____

_____

_____

_____

_____

What words have you felt were insignificant but later realized their importance?

_____

_____

_____

_____

_____

_____

_____

_____

_____

The Gospel Series

For easy, compact, but profound studies to teach to others, information and resources can all be found at https://www.igobible-study.com/copy-of-bevel-your-bible.

You can also email me for modified versions of this series.

What is "The Gospel?" Let's start there. Most people know it as "the good news," great! WHAT IS "the Good News"?

Check this out. It's the
- DEATH,
- BURIAL, AND
- RESURRECTION.

Great, but the Bible says that we have to OBEY THE GOSPEL. How do I obey what he has already done?

DEATH: Repentance
BURIAL: Baptism in Jesus's Name
RESURRECTION: Receive the Holy Ghost with evidence of speaking in tongues.

Mark 16:15 and, "he said unto them, Go ye into all the world, and preach the gospel to every creature. He that believeth and is baptized shall be saved; but he that believeth not shall be damned."

Salvation scriptures are not to scare us into heaven, but they are to help us understand the commission of the apostles/disciples and our role in this life.

Take the time to read the following information and be ready to obey it, teach it and spread the good news!

110 MILES WITH JESUS

What is Faith? (Hebrews 11:1, Ephesians 2:8)

Who is Jesus? (John 1:1–14, Exodus 6:2–3, John 8:58)

What is the Gospel? (2 Timothy 3:16; Acts 2:38, 8:12–17)

Why do we repent? (Luke 13:3, Acts 3:19, Mark 1:4)

How do we get baptized? (Matthew 28:19)

When do we receive the Holy Ghost? (John 14:18, Acts 2:17, Joel 2:28, John 14:26)

Four Words

Humbleness, obedience, sacrifice, and promises.

Another year has passed. Another New Year's Eve is about to come and go. I am praying. I am reflecting. I've made progress. I am praying for what is to come this new year. God shows up and speaks, "When you humble yourself, are fully obedient, and sacrifice all that you have, the promises I have given will come to pass."

To go into all that had happened during the months following would take another book. Some are not to be shared. Some are personal. Some are embarrassing. Some of my perspective of my experiences would be hurtful to others, if shared. Some are already written in this book. Just know that I did my very best that particular year to be exactly what those first three words required of me. Because of my efforts, God showed up, showed out, and blessed our family more than we could have ever imagined!

Promises Were Fulfilled!

When you can get to a place with God and your leaders where you can be open and honest with them, humble yourself to the point of embarrassment, and give sacrificially of your time, efforts, and emotions, God will bless you. He will fulfill promises that have already been written in his word, as well as promises spoken over you by others and by himself.

Allow God to take you through a process of brokenness in order to piece you back together for a good purpose.

110 MILES WITH JESUS

What is a theme or a word that you can follow for the coming year?

_____

_____

_____

_____

_____

Things that line up with that theme or word throughout the year.

January

_____

_____

_____

_____

_____

February

_____

_____

_____

_____

_____

March

_____

_____

_____

_____

_____

MARLO COKER

April

May

June

This Is How We Drive

Lord! Lord! LORD! LORD!

He's going to kill us!

"Stop being dramatic. You're fine. He's not going to kill you. He's a good driver. He's not going to let anything happen to his family."

Well, tell him to SLOW DOWN!

Just at that moment, as if hubby could hear my conversation with God. Most likely, it was the gasps as I winced. He looked over at me and said, "THIS IS HOW WE DRIVE HERE!"

"What do you mean 'we,' you've only been here for two weeks! You don't even live here yet!"

"But we will be living here, and we can't be driving around like we're scared. We have to be ready to merge into their culture."

(Oh, so now you have HIM teaching me lessons? Okay, Lord.)

We are in the world, but we are not of the world. We don't have to try to fit in, but we do have to be willing to drive a little faster or eat specific foods in order to be involved in the culture. We can't walk around with our heads down and act like we're scared to move around in an area that we were called to.

If we're scared, we're never going to talk to the person that needs a church card. *We will never go into that one store for the purpose of telling our testimony to the man who is so unsure of his choices.* We can be cautious and use wisdom. We can also be bold and know that we have the authority to step on the enemy's head and crush it!

You're not going to die. He's not going to kill you, and he's not going to let anything happen to his children who walk in obedience and authority!

What is the most frightening scenario you can think of that makes it hard for you to witness to someone?

How can you combat your fear of witnessing to others?

What's the Difference?

After a weeklong trip to St. Louis, Missouri, I was driving back home to the mountains of Georgia. I looked up, and just at the farthest sight, I could see them!

"MY mountains! They're so beautiful!"

GOD: Excuse me? YOUR mountains?
ME: Well, I guess you gave us dominion over the earth, right? (I could feel a lesson.)
GOD: Yes, I gave you DOMINION, not POSSESSION.
I felt the door slam in my face. This meant homework.

Possession Dominion

Noun, Noun.

Control or occupancy of power or the use of power; sovereignty over something for which one does not over something stewardship, supremacy. Necessarily have private property rights, something that is owned. I praised and honored him that liveth forever, whose dominion is an everlasting dominion, a territory under the rule of Daniel 4:34 another country.

The condition or affliction of "To choose between dominion being possessed by a demon or slavery," Benjamin Jowett, or other supernatural entity, English scholar.

One who possesses is often an order of angels in Christianity said to have possession (of), angelology, ranked above "hold possession (of)," or be angels and below thrones. In possession (of) Colossians 1:16.

Are you still confused? So was I.

Possession is a related term of dominion.

As a noun, possession is a control or occupancy of something for which one does not necessarily have private property rights.

As a verb, possession is (obsolete) to invest with property.

As a proper noun, dominion is any of the self-governing nations of the British commonwealth.

Dominion works with possession ONLY WHEN we are obedient to the Holy Spirit!

Joshua 1: (possession)

Joshua 23:5–10: (obedience, courage, faith)

First Corinthians 15:49–58: (inheritance which leads to possession, but not dominion…yet)

Genesis 1:26–27: (dominion)

God has full dominion over everything, and he has given us this land for the purpose of possession. However, when we operate in the Holy Ghost, we have the same authority that he has. Therefore, we can now take dominion over situations but not over the land because we don't belong to this world. We belong to Jesus, and one day, we will belong in heaven.

Onomatopoeia

Kapow! Zap! Bang! Have you ever had those days where you feel like everything is just YUCK? Life is just throwing you one punch after another.

The term "misery love company," as long as I've heard it, has always meant, "If I'm miserable, I want you to be miserable with me" or "I'm going to hang around others who are just as miserable as me."

A particularly difficult situation in our family that lasted months caused me to want to be an ostrich digging my head in a hole in the sand. I handled my obligatory responsibilities, but other than that, I dealt with people as little as possible.

HOWEVER, one Sunday, I forced myself to get up early and walk with friends. I went to church. I met and chatted with friends.

I worshipped.

I cried.

I prayed.

In the middle of the day, I started to feel better! In prayer today, the Lord spoke to me.

"Misery Loves Company"

WHAT, LORD?

"Misery Loves Company"

Not in the sense that we're used to thinking. It's easy to hide yourself when life gets you down. It's easy to avoid everything and everyone. It's easy to keep yourself in the dark.

It's hard to face people while you're struggling. It's hard to face your problems in the daylight.

BUT when you get yourself around people who love you, support you, and want to see that joy that GOD gave you, it's easy to be with people!

It's easy to be in good company.

My misery loves your company because when I'm around you and when I'm in God's presence and with like-minded friends, my misery dissipates and turns into joy!

110 MILES WITH JESUS

That day, I
- "made" friendship,
- "made" prayer,
- "made" worship,
- "made" praise,
- "made" fellowship.

When you're feeling low or antisocial, call a friend and invite them to coffee or to your home to sit and chat with you; WHO?

Praying Through the Temple

GOD: Time for a fast (all smirky-like).

ME: I do fast every week.

GOD: Time for a cleansing fast.

Me: Oooohh, okay. Starting when?

God: Two days from now.

ME: Oh, good. I have time to prepare my body for a ten-day fast.

GOD: Whoa…who said ten days?

ME: Well, I want to honor you. I can do it.

GOD: Seven days, starting Saturday, ending Friday.

ME: Can I do ten and end it Sunday with communion?

God: Seven days, you will end it with communion. Saturday to Friday.

ME: Okay, prep time begins!

Preparation Days

> Howbeit this kind goeth not out but by prayer and fasting. (Matthew 17:21)

Before I enter into this time, I will have a COMPLETE understanding of why I'm doing this and know that God has called me to this for a purpose. I am warring against a spirit, and I CANNOT win this battle without prayer AND fasting. The Lord has given me the Tabernacle plan as my map to guide me. I have been sitting outside the camp, willing to participate in the building and materials but now I am ready to enter in.

> Make a joyful noise unto the LORD, all ye lands. Serve the LORD with gladness: Come before his presence with singing. Know ye that the LORD he is God: It is he that hath made us, and not we ourselves; We are his people, and the sheep of his pasture. Enter into his gates with

thanksgiving, And into his courts with praise: Be thankful unto him, and bless his name. For the LORD is good; his mercy is everlasting; And his truth endureth to all generations. (**Psalm 100**)

Before I walk into the Tabernacle, I have to come making a JOYFUL noise! I have to immediately recognize what I'm doing and why. I am Christ's, and I am not my own. He has called me to this, and I am his sheep! I will be thankful to him for allowing me to graze in his land! Now I will walk into his Tabernacle with purpose and specific direction.

And I set my face unto the Lord God, to seek by prayer and supplications, with fasting, and sackcloth and ashes. (**Daniel 9:3**)

Questions to ask while preparing.

What can I do differently in prayer and position during this time?

_____

_____

_____

_____

_____

_____

How can my focus in prayer be shifted this day?

_____

_____

_____

_____

_____

_____

What does my attitude look like in prayer? How do I want to approach God?

What do I need to sacrifice in order for God to replenish? What does that look like spiritually and physically?

What needs to die in my life?

Why am I putting on a sackcloth, fasting for what? Starting with the inward and then the outward.

Fasting While Praying Through the Temple

Day 1: Face unto the Lord God
Brazen Altar: Repentance
Brazen Laver: Word of God
Day 2: Praying at the Five Pillars
Wonderful
Counselor
Mighty God
Everlasting Father
Prince of Peace
Day 3: Supplications: Holy Ghost
My attitude is the way that these things will come to pass. I
will stay humble in his presence.
Day 4: Fasting at the Table of Shewbread.
Pray for your leaders and pastor.
Empty yourself of anything unclean.
Allow the present and past words to fill you when you feel
hungry.
Day 5: Ashes, Altar of Incense
What needs to die in my life?
Day 6: Four Pillars, Ark of the Covenant Contents (sackcloth)
The Four Pillars of Matthew, Mark, Luke, and John, repen-
tance/submission, grief, self-humiliation Ark of the
Covenant/Mercy Seat Content Garment—rough mate-
rial, do hard things
Ten Commandments: The voice of God, instructions, and
Holy Ghost Manna—the daily word.
Aaron's Rod: grief, humiliation.
Day 7: Come out of the Tabernacle with Praise!
I broke my fast with communion because the Lord instructed
me to. This was a personal direction, not one that was
required to break a fast.

A note on fasting.

Fasting, like most sacrificial behaviors, is between you and God. We fast in order to get closer to God, not to get things from him. A fast can be one meal, one day, one week. It can be abstaining from food, only water, or a specific food item. It could be social media, whatever it is that you feel is hindering your walk with God or distracting you from your purpose, fast THAT. If you are doing an extended fast, discuss it with your spouse and pastor. They may be able to give you direction and be in prayer with you to block any spiritual attacks while you fast.

Anthony Mangun's prayer through the Tabernacle is powerful! I recommend using this video. Https://youtu.be/vHjvBg-aRNo?si=Bt3vD9nTjutnLVFy

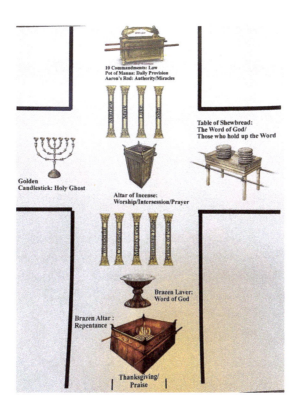

Absence Makes the What Do What?

Have you heard the term,

"Absence make the heart grow fonder."

If it's supposed to be related to young love, maybe I can understand. Related to a twenty-five-year marriage where we've come to depend on each other and know our roles? No! Absence creates chaos, frustration, and tears! I need my husband HOME! He's been gone for over two weeks. I need a face-to-face conversation. I need him to do stuff.

I need (ehem, children close your ears) intimacy.

GOD: *This is how I feel about my bride. I need to have conversations with them. I need them to do stuff. I need up close and personal intimacy with them.*

Absence from God is dangerous. It creates lust for other things in this world, and it creates a hindrance from his work being done.

Draw nigh to God, and he will draw nigh to you. (James 4:8)

For I am persuaded, that neither death, nor life, nor angels, nor principalities, nor powers, nor things present, nor things to come, nor height, nor depth, nor any other creature, shall be able to separate us from the love of God, which is in Christ Jesus our Lord. (Romans 8:38–39)

Where in this triangle does your relationship with Jesus fall?

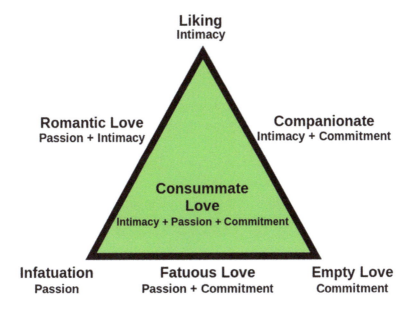

How can you make your relationship fall into the center of the triangle?

_____
_____
_____
_____
_____
_____
_____
_____
_____
_____
_____
_____
_____
_____
_____
_____
_____

Get Your House Ready

OOOHHHH, something good is about to go down tonight, Lord! I feel it as I'm driving to this revival service! You're about to do SOMETHING!

There was a revival service at another church in the area that my pastor encouraged us to go to the night before, and it was amazing. When the home Pastor announced that they were adding another night, I asked our Pastor if I could go back. Of course! So I did! That man of God who visited obeyed the Holy Ghost at the altar. First, he walked right passed me as I was worshiping, and then he stopped in his tracks, turned to me, and spoke,

> *The Holy Ghost sent me to tell you that the prayers you have been praying for over nine years are about to be answered. Get your house ready to receive the promises. The Holy Ghost sent me to tell you the prayers that you have been praying for those that have been running are the prayers that have been keeping death from their door. Get ready for your house to receive the promise. It looks like chaos and destruction at the moment but get ready for the promises.*

There is no way he could have known the time frame of our prayers or what I have been praying. The Lord sent someone to help build my faith when it was ALMOST shattered.

Bonus note: Do NOT miss an opportunity to be in the house of God. You may just miss a direct word from the Lord.

110 MILES WITH JESUS

What is something that you have been praying about that has caused your faith to fail?

_____

_____

_____

_____

_____

_____

_____

_____

When has the Lord shown you a promise not yet fulfilled but has directed you to keep believing for it?

_____

_____

_____

_____

_____

_____

_____

Let us draw near with a true heart in *full assurance of faith*, having our hearts sprinkled from an evil conscience, and our bodies washed with pure water. Let us hold fast the *profession of our faith without wavering;* (for he is faithful that promised;) and let us consider one another to provoke unto love and to good works: not forsaking the *assembling of ourselves together*, as the manner of some is; but exhorting one another: and so much the more, as ye see the day approaching. (Hebrews 10:22–25)

How Much Longer?

Me: (6:00 a.m. and just starting my drive to work) God, how long am I going to do this drive? I mean, I'm okay with the paycheck and the opportunity, but I'm tired! I wake up earlier than the worms that the birds eat, and I drive further than Abraham walked. I'm tired.

God:

Me: Hello?! Are you there?

God:

Me: Okay. I'm sorry. You are amazing, and your plan is perfect. I will do all things for your name and your honor. Thank you for every opportunity.

God: Good morning. Do not be weary in well doing. Your steps are ordered.

Me: Thank you, and good morning to you.

That was roughly two weeks before I got a month's notice that my student was going to be moving districts, and I would not be following them due to added distance. Instead of being relieved about not having to drive so far or get up so early, now I'm panicking because I have NO JOB!

God: *Your steps are ordered. Stop relying on the world to sustain you. I sustain you. I will take care of you.*

He gave me a new job. He provided for us, and even though my income was sliced into a fourth of what I was making, my budget knew no difference.

When we don't depend on this world for our happiness, our finances, or our self-worth, God has room to show just how much he wants to bless us.

> Peace I leave with you, my peace I give unto you: not as the world giveth, give I unto you. Let not your heart be troubled, neither let it be afraid. (John 14:27)

110 MILES WITH JESUS

What, from this world, are you relying too much on?

How can God prove to you that he is faithful in his provision?

When you pray today, read *Psalm 20*, and listen to *"Tis So Sweet to Trust in Jesus"* By Casting Crowns.

Time to Get Uncomfortable

I love newness! I don't mind change AT ALL! So walking onto a new job does not bother me. I also love learning new things and learning about new people. I feel like I've never met a stranger, BUT THIS PLACE IS SCARY, LORD!

Everyone is mad or tired or?

God: They're sad. And they're frustrated. They're hurt. They need me.

Me: What am I to do? Even HER, I'm scared of her. She's angry.

God: She's sad. She's frustrated. She's worried. Pray for her.

Me: Help me to show her grace and mercy where I have already received it. Help me to show YOUR love, not like I would give it, but like YOU would give it. In return, can I get a little favor? (Eyes batting with a grin.)

God: (Smiles with a slight wink.)

From that day on, I felt what they felt. I felt how God felt about them. I did my best to show mercy, grace, and love in each situation, even when it was hard. I smiled when I wanted to cry. I stayed when I wanted to leave. God showed up in that place. He made his presence known in multiple ways. He showed up in conversations, even when he wasn't necessarily welcomed by all. He showed favor, even when it wasn't deserved. He made the uncomfortable bearable and even joyful at times.

Continuing the conversation later in the weeks. "And by the way, it's only temporary. You're not gonna be there for very long, but while you are there. Keep doing what you're doing.

I'm proud of you" (God).

Imagine what you bring into your workplace. Imagine how your joy and God's mercy and favor can change an environment. Imagine God looking at you and saying, "Well done, thy good and faithful servant!"

What can you do, even when it's hard to bring the love of God into your workplace?

Look at Me!

Lorcl, I need you. I need you to send someone to confirm what I'm feeling in my spirit. I need you to help me sort all these emotions out. I don't want to do anything hasty based on emotion. I want to know that it's right and that it's in your will, not my own. Send someone to tell me.

This was on a car ride to our home church. I wanted something, I felt something shift in my spirit and I needed confirmation that it was right. I cried about it. I prayed about it, but I did not tell anyone how or what I was feeling (except my husband). I wanted to know that IF something was spoken out loud, it was because GOD told them to speak it and not because I told them how I was feeling.

As we attended our home church service, there was no confirmation in the preaching. As the altar service was called, there was no one who came to pray with us to confirm what I was feeling. NOTHING WAS SPOKEN.

As I was catching up with friends, my home pastor's wife came to me, hugged me, and asked, "How are you? How is everything going?"

Without hesitation and with a not-so-real but not completely fake smile, I said, "We're good!"

I wasn't lying because, with God, everything is good. But I looked into her eyes, and I stared into her soul, not like a creep, but just long enough to see if she could read my mind, my spirit, my angst, whatever. I waited for her to say what I wanted her to say, but SHE DIDN'T.

She simply said, "That's great. We are praying for you guys."

There were other words in between and after that were shared, but those are private. The point is that I was looking for a spoken word, but it didn't happen. We hugged, said our goodbyes, and headed back home, disappointed, frustrated, and sad.

I thought God was ignoring my request.

110 MILES WITH JESUS

A short time later, God sent someone. Completely unexpected. He wasn't ignoring me! He just did it in HIS fashion and not mine!

It's okay to tell God how you're feeling. It's okay to tell him what you want. It's okay to ask for confirmation as long as it's from reliable sources. Understand that it may not be answered or at least not answered in the way that you expect it. Look at Gideon, he asked God each day to dampen or dry the wool fleece in order to confirm what the Spirit already told him.

Gideon tested God instead of trusted his word, but God still answered. He proved himself in order to save the nation. (Read the story of Gideon and all of the confirmations of his word in Judges 6.)

Have you felt an angst in your spirit?

_____

_____

_____

_____

_____

_____

_____

_____

How can you ask God to confirm his word to you?

_____

_____

_____

_____

_____

_____

_____

_____

Who do you think he will send to speak into your life?

Come back later to journal when that word is confirmed. Is it what or who you thought it was?

God Is on the Move

ARE YOU SERIOUS RIGHT NOW?

"You sold my house in less than forty-eight hours of it being on the market? What kind of craziness is THAT?"

GOD: I told you. Things were going to change. I told you not to get comfortable. More importantly, I told you to MOVE!

ME: I know, we are. I'm trying to be obedient, and faithful, and excited. I'm just AGGGGHH!

God: I know. Do you remember what I told you when I told you to move to Florida?

ME: Yes, "Go to Florida with your husband. I will lead your path. I will be with you. I will not leave you."

GOD: Go to Detroit, you and your husband. I will lead your paths, individually and collectively. I will be with you all. I will not leave any of you.

ME: Okay. Here we go! AGAIN! By the way, YOU'RE AMAZING, and I love you! **So much!**

GOD: I love you too, SO MUCH!

> **Order my steps in thy word: And let not any iniquity have dominion over me. (Psalm 119:133)**

110 MILES WITH JESUS

When has God given you a word for one situation many years ago that still applies to a current situation? Even if it sounds just a little different?

When have you had a hard time seeing the FULL plan come together, yet in hindsight, you see it so clearly?

Withhold Nothing

"May 13, right, Lord? I gave my notice at work, ending May 9. I'm packing stuff up. I'm following the plan."

GOD: Are you?

ME: What do you mean?

GOD: Is it YOUR timing or MINE?

ME: Well, by my calculations, we close on the twenty-fourth, and I graduate on the tenth, so it just makes sense for me to work up until my graduation.

GOD: So your timing.

ME: Well, yeah. When am I supposed to go?

GOD: Change your notice to the eighteenth. Help your husband with the house. I'm going to give you some rest when he leaves. You stay until your last exam.

ME: So May 1?

God: Yes.

ME: And our son? Are you going to take care of him (as tears start to fall)?

GOD: Now I know that you will withhold NOTHING from me. You have given your home, your job, your plans, and both of your son's futures. Watch what happens next!

Just like Abraham, when we give our sacrifice, even when we know it will hurt. God provides.

What is something that is hard to give up, to the point of hurt?

When we open our hands to give instead of to receive, God blesses us more than we can imagine!
What does your "withhold nothing" look like?

God Roar

"Well, that was a sobering church service. I'm not mad, God. I'm just sad. I'm excited to move and the new things, but WHAT ABOUT OUR SONS? WE'RE JUST GOING TO LEAVE THEM FURTHER SOUTH WHILE WE GO FURTHER NORTH?"

GOD: DO YOU TRUST ME?
ME: Yes, but—
GOD: DO YOU TRUST ME?
ME: Yes. But I don't want to talk anymore.
GOD: Play "Lion" by Elevation Worship.
ME: Wow, that was powerful!
God: Play "God Roar" by Denee Richardson.

As the song was playing, we pulled into the garage, and the sound was just blaring through the metal and concrete. Hubby and Mom got out of the car. I sat there, turned it up, and cried. I can't even tell you if I said anything to the Lord. But I know I cried. When the song was over, I could have put it on repeat and cried through it again, but I trusted that God heard my heart and the words of "God Roar," which resonated with what was in my heart. I left it in his hands because **I TRUSTED HIM.** I wiped the tears from my face, cleaned it up a little, and got out of the car with my head held high.

110 MILES WITH JESUS

What song do you play that you know God can hear your heart through the lyrics?

Make your prayer list here.

Remember, he wants them back more than you do!

Entertaining Angels Unaware

Wake up!
"Lord, what time is it? 4:30 a.m.? Why! (rolls back over)"
Wake up!
"Okay! Sheesh. Can I make some coffee?"
"Yes, but go outside to drink it."
"Seriously? At 4:30? In Sixty degrees? In the pitch-black dark?"
"Yes! Yes! Yes! Yes!"
"And Pray."

I sit outside.
Coffee in hand.
Blanket on lap.
Sleep booger in eyes.
I begin to pray softly.
I lift my hands toward the sky and into darkness.
Tears fall again.
I'm so tired of crying.
I pray for the boys.
I pray for the area.
I pray for our soon-to-be "old" church.
I pray for our soon-to-be "new" church.
I pray for the son that I feel like I'm abandoning.
I pray for the son that I feel like I've already abandoned.
Dawn has broken.
The Son is up.
I go back inside. Time for work. Lunch break.

My son came back!

Apr 15, 11:13 AM

Kevin

Evin just spoke in tongues a good renewing

Devine appointment at Tom the Rv rental

Thank you so much for being obedient to Gods Spirit today. He has been calling the pastor of our old church, and the pastor of the new church. You were spot on, not knowing anything about us. I do believe that was a Devine appointment. And a come to JESUS moment. I am blessed that God sent a complete stranger to give a Word. And to renew him in the Holy Ghost. Again I am so thankful that you allowed God to flow instead of holding back. We all need to let the Spirit flow through us and not let our flesh get in the way. God Bless you and your wife.

I think he will never forget that God sent a stranger to speak into him.

Had I not seen the complete transformation when I got home, I would not have believed it for myself! People who barely know him saw a picture of him on Facebook and said, "He looks so happy." He was changed in an instant!

HALLELUJAH! THANK YOU! HALLELUJAH!

God: There's more

Me: I know, you promised my other son would come back one day. I'll still be prayerful and still be thankful.

God: Yes, but there's more. You now have a burden, a responsibility to pray for the ones that haven't come home yet.

Me: OKAY! You and me, we'll do it together with others.

God: Yes, you are not alone. You are a partner with others I have called.

"Are you one that he has called to intercede for others?"

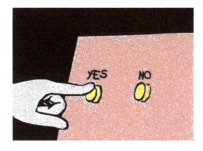

Don't Be Afraid of Their Faces

Hubby is in Detroit searching for a house with the criteria I asked for at least two bedrooms and two bathrooms, a garage would be nice, move-in ready would be nice, and safe area is a MUST.

Oh, and be sure to keep it under $150,000. He is frustrated because the market is not allowing him to meet the criteria, especially the SAFE part. He wanted to be near the water, outside the city limits. I didn't care if we were in the city or out, just as long as it was safe.

I'm in Georgia, working and doing all of the things. Sunday service, getting ready to wind down altar/prayer service toward the end. Here's God showing out again,

> Don't be afraid to walk through a land that I have called you to. Do not be afraid of their faces! I have sent angels to go before you. I have sent angels to go behind you, and I am walking beside you! DO NOT BE AFRAID TO WALK THROUGH THE LAND THAT I HAVE CALLED YOU TO! DO NOT BE AFRAID OF THEIR FACES (mic drop). (God)

Hubby had been looking at a house that was out of budget and in a questionable location—inner city but close to outer city. I compromised on raising the purchase price, and hubby compromised on location. This is the house we bought. The first time I rode through the area and walked through the house, I was ALL IN—no doubts or red flags.

Pastor's wife called me when she went to look at it, "You're definitely in the inner city! Don't be afraid of their faces. Look at God at work!"

The day I moved up here, as I drove through the city, I could now see the inner cities. But I wasn't afraid. I was excited! I could feel the hunger and the Holy Ghost opportunity!

Just like those that are mentioned in the "hall of faith" in Hebrews, chapter 11. We walk by faith. It sustains us. It helps us realize that while there are questionable situations, we are not alone in our journey. He will protect us!

What is something that God has called you to where you had to say, "Lord, I believe; help thou mine unbelief."

_____

_____

_____

_____

_____

_____

_____

_____

_____

_____

How do you shake that fear and doubt out of your mind in order to see God's plan carried out?

_____

_____

_____

_____

_____

_____

_____

_____

_____

_____

_____

Homework

READ HEBREWS CHAPTER 11 (vs. 8 tells me that promises come after obedience).

Thy Will

On the way to the prayer room, I start thinking about all the things and people I need to pray for. I mentally make my laundry list of how I'm going to fill my time—my obligatory duty. I walk into the very edge of the prayer room, and the Holy Ghost pretty much smacks me right in the face.

I found a seat as quickly as I possibly could to recover from the assault so I can start praying my predetermined prayers. As soon as I open my mouth, I start speaking in tongues.

> Likewise the Spirit also helpeth our infirmities: for we know not what we should pray for as we ought: but the Spirit itself maketh intercession for us with groanings which cannot be uttered. And he that searcheth the hearts knoweth what is the mind of the Spirit, because he maketh intercession for the saints **according to the will of God.** (Romans 8:26–27)

And there it was, everything that I planned to pray. My whole list went out the window, and every time I began to speak in any form of an English word, the only thing that would come out was,

Thy Will Be Done

I walked out of that prayer room (hours later) approximately ten feet taller. I knew that God was up to something, and he sure was! There were some amazing things that happened from 2019–2024. If you know me, you know the stories; if you don't know me, follow me on social media, and you can read all about them all!

Your turn. Write down all of your plans, prayers, hopes, and dreams. Go on and do it. I'll wait.

You're done? Good.

Now take a black Sharpie and scribble it all out!

Because God already has a plan. He doesn't need your opinion! He just wants to talk to you, and he wants you to talk to him, not tell you what your plans are.

Have a nice day!

About the Author

This is the second published book by Marlo Coker. Her first book, *Jesus Stole My Weed!: A Testimony of Substance Abuse Freedom (and Other Life-Altering Stories)* cowritten with her husband, Kevin Coker. She enjoys writing testimonies and experiences with Jesus throughout her life. She has kept a journal of major experiences and testimonies with Jesus as well as written several unpublished Bible studies that apply to her daily life. She enjoys talking about the word of God and being with those who are of like-minded faith. Since she has found God, she has had opportunities to travel across the nation as well as different countries and has enjoyed meeting people from various cultures. Her passion for most things is portrayed in her writings.

www.ingramcontent.com/pod-product-compliance
Lightning Source LLC
Chambersburg PA
CBHW060844310125
21141CB00053B/949